ACONCAGUA

AND THE SOUTHERN ANDES

I grew up in this city, my poetry was born between the mountain and the river, it took its voice from the rain, and like the timber, it steeped itself in the forests.

Pablo Neruda (Chilean Poet)

About the author

Jim Ryan is a civil engineer by profession. A seasoned traveller, his lifelong passion for the mountains has taken him to many remote places. He has travelled, and written extensively, on some of the great walks of the world, such as in Nepal, Lesotho in South Africa, Kilimanjaro and the island of Reunion in the Indian Ocean. His guidebooks include *Carrauntoohil and The MacGillycuddy Reeks* and *Scenic Walks in Killarney*, as well as *The Mountains of Nerja*, published by Cicerone.

Jim has a special interest in geology. The mountain of Aconcagua and its region made a significant impression on him on his first journey there as part of an expedition in 1999/2000. He noted the lack of information on one of the world's great mountains and produced this guidebook. This is the third update on the original issue.

Acknowledgements

Thanks are due to Fergus Humphries for producing the maps, to Eduardo Depetris, Pablo Reguera, Sebastian Tetilla, Angel Tetilla, Marco Garrido Dasté, Pedro Marzolo, Nito Giordano, Pancho Medina, Elias Lira, Gisela Palacios, Heber Orona, and to Professor John Gamble of University College Cork. Thanks to Quazi Shahriar Rahman for the picture of the Cólera campsite, to Arkaitz Mendia Arakama for the photo from the summit down the Canaleta, and to Xabi 'Smithy' Mujika for the pictures of Camp Guanacos, the Grande Acarreo and Camp Cólera. For this latest revision to the guide I was accompanied by my son, Dylan, and by my partner, Birgit Halir, both of whom I am indebted to for their support and patience.

ACONCAGUA
AND THE SOUTHERN ANDES

by Jim Ryan

CICERONE

JUNIPER HOUSE, MURLEY MOSS,
OXENHOLME ROAD, KENDAL, CUMBRIA LA9 7RL
www.cicerone.co.uk

© Jim Ryan 2018
Third edition 2018
ISBN: 978 1 85284 974 0
Second edition 2009
First edition 2004

Printed in China on behalf of Latitude Press Ltd
A catalogue record for this book is available from the British Library.
All photographs are by the author unless otherwise stated.

Warning

Mountaineering and mountain walking can be a dangerous activity carrying a risk of personal injury or death. It should be undertaken only by those with a full understanding of the risks and with the training and experience to evaluate them. While every care and effort has been taken in the preparation of this guide, the user should be aware that conditions can be highly variable and can change quickly, materially affecting the seriousness of a climb or expedition.

The mountains described in this book reach high altitudes. There are health risks in high-altitude climbing such as pulmonary and cerebral oedema (which can cause sickness and death); extreme temperatures (which can cause frostbite); and traversing over ice (risk of falling and sliding). Climbers are advised to be in good physical condition; to acclimatise and not too ascend too quickly; to keep a constant check on saturated oxygen level; to descend if they feel unwell; to consult a doctor before attempting high-altitude climbs; and to bring adequate medication, gear and clothing with them. Training in ice climbing, ropework and high-altitude problems is essential for the uninitiated.

Therefore, except for any liability that cannot be excluded by law, neither Cicerone nor the author accept liability for damage of any nature (including damage to property, personal injury or death) arising directly or indirectly from the information in this book.

Front cover: The route to Plaza Argentina (Vacas Valley Route)

CONTENTS

INDEX OF MAPS AND ILLUSTRATIONS

Updates to this Guide

While every effort is made by our authors to ensure the accuracy of guidebooks as they go to print, changes can occur during the lifetime of an edition. Please check the Cicerone website (www.cicerone.co.uk/974/updates) for any updates before planning your trip. We also advise that you check information about such things as transport, accommodation and shops locally. Even rights of way can be altered over time.

The route maps in this guide are derived from publicly-available data, databases and crowd-sourced data. As such they have not been through the detailed checking procedures that would generally be applied to a published map from an official mapping agency, although naturally we have reviewed them closely in the light of local knowledge as part of the preparation of this guide. We are always grateful for information about any discrepancies between a guidebook and the facts on the ground, sent by email to updates@cicerone.co.uk or by post to Cicerone, Juniper House, Murley Moss, Oxenholme Road, Kendal, LA9 7RL, United Kingdom.

Register your book: To sign up to receive free updates, special offers and GPX files where available, register your book at www.cicerone.co.uk.

Map key

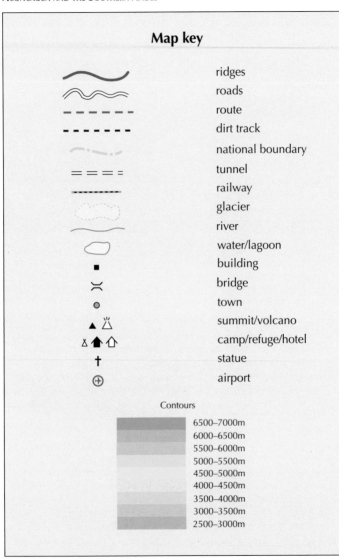

	ridges
	roads
	route
	dirt track
	national boundary
	tunnel
	railway
	glacier
	river
	water/lagoon
	building
	bridge
	town
	summit/volcano
	camp/refuge/hotel
	statue
	airport

Contours

6500–7000m
6000–6500m
5500–6000m
5000–5500m
4500–5000m
4000–4500m
3500–4000m
3000–3500m
2500–3000m

Map of South America

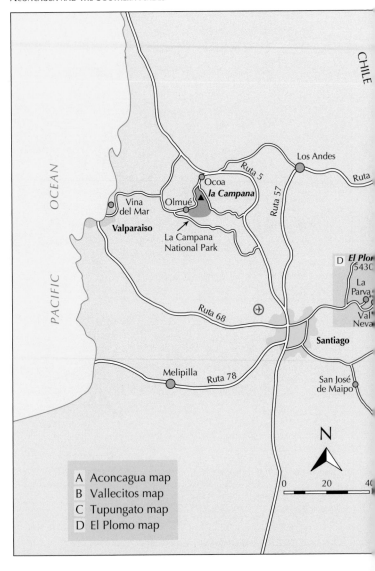

A Aconcagua map
B Vallecitos map
C Tupungato map
D El Plomo map

Area maps in this guide

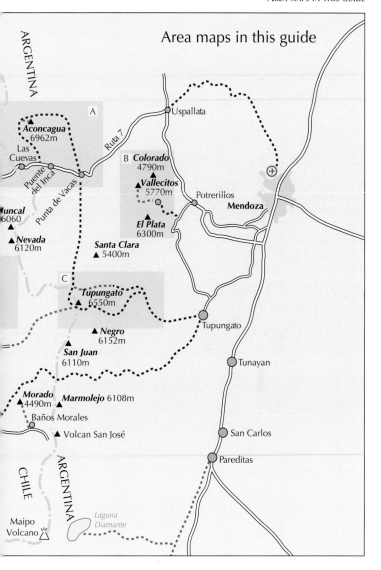

ARGENTINA

A

Aconcagua
6962m

Las Cuevas

Puente del Inca

Punta de Vacas

Ruta 7

Uspallata

B **Colorado**
4790m

▲**Vallecitos**
5770m

Potrerillos

Mendoza

El Plata
6300m

uncal
6060

▲**Nevada**
6120m

Santa Clara
▲ 5400m

C

Tupungato
▲ 6550m

▲ **Negro**
6152m

San Juan
6110m

Tupungato

Tunayan

Morado
▲4490m **Marmolejo** 6108m

Baños Morales

▲ Volcan San José

San Carlos

Pareditas

CHILE

ARGENTINA

Maipo
Volcano ⛰

Laguna Diamante

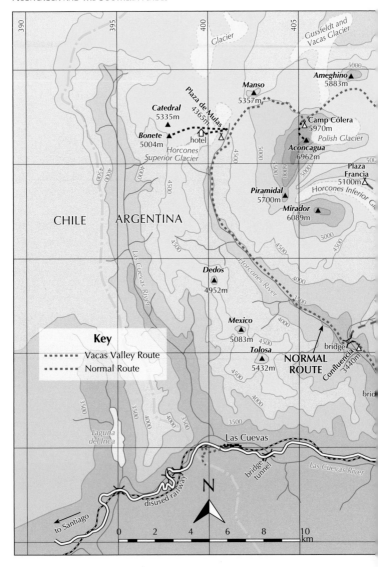

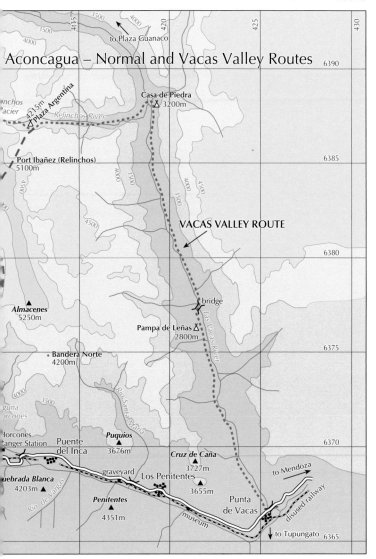

Aconcagua – Normal and Vacas Valley Routes

to Plaza Guanaco

6390

inchos
acier

Plaza Argentina
4215m

Relinchos River

Casa de Piedra
✕ 3200m

Port Ibañez (Relinchos)
5100m

6385

4000

3500

4500

VACAS VALLEY ROUTE

6380

✕ bridge

Almacenes
5250m

Las Vacas River

Pampa de Leñas ✕
2800m

6375

▲ Bandera Norte
4200m

Rio Santa María

4000

3500

guna
rcones

6370

Horcones
anger Station

Puente
del Inca

Puquios ▲
3676m

Cruz de Caña ▲
3727m

to Mendoza

disused railway

graveyard
Los Penitentes

▲
3655m

Punta
de Vacas

uebrada Blanca
4203m ▲

Rio de Vargas

Penitentes
▲
4351m

museum

to Tupungato 6365

13

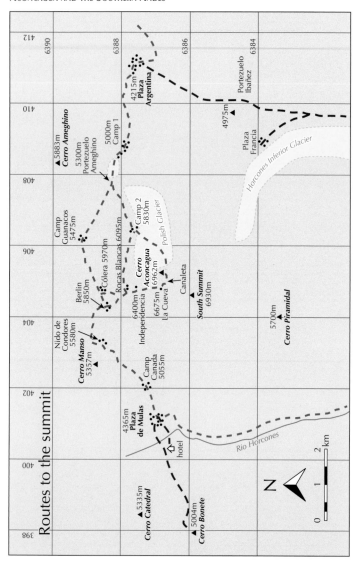

Routes to the summit

SUMMARY OF CAMPS – NORMAL ROUTE

Camp	Elev	Elev Gain	Distance	Time	Difficulties
Roadhead Horcones	2535	-	-	-	Present permit and passport at Ranger Station
Confluencia	3420	885m	8km	2½ hrs	Easy walk. Hot, no shade
Basecamp Plaza de Mulas	4365	945m	28km	8 hrs	Tough, long day. May have to cross shallow streams. Wind-blown sand. No shade
Canada	5055	690m	3km	5 hrs	Steep, steady climb
Nido de Condores	5580	525m	4km	5 hrs	Steep, steady climb
Cólera	5970	390m	5km	4½ hrs	Tough, though short, climb
Summit	6962	992m	9km	9 hrs	Long trek, initially in the dark, very cold. Canaleta the most difficult part. Descent to Cólera will take 5 hours
Return to Basecamp			12km	6 hrs	Steep in places
Return to Roadhead			36km	9 hrs	Long, energy-sapping walk

SUMMARY OF CAMPS – VACAS VALLEY ROUTE

Camp	Elev	Elev Gain	Distance	Time	Difficulties
Roadhead Punta de Vacas	2415	-	-	-	Present permit and passport at Ranger Station
Pampa de Leñas	2800	385m	18km	5 hrs	Medium grade, though undulating, pleasant beside river
Casa de Piedra	3200	400m	17km	5 hrs	Similar to previous day
Basecamp Plaza Argentina	4215	1015m	12km	7 hrs	Cross ice-cold river, then precipitous walk, cross a second river. Steep initially. Steady/medium thereafter
Camp 1	5000	785m	3km	5 hrs	Tough climb through penitentes
Guanacos	5475	475m	4km	6 hrs	Initially tough climb possibly in crampons through snow/ice. Then easy walk
Cólera	5970	495m	4km	4 hrs	Tough, though short, climb
Summit	6962	992m	9km	9 hours	Long trek, initially in the dark, very cold. Canaleta the most difficult part. Descent to Cólera will take 5 hours
Return to Basecamp			20km	7 hours	Long and steep descent, especially coming into basecamp
Return to Roadhead			47km	2 days 9 hours + 4½ hrs	First day is very long to Pampa de Leñas. Two rivers to cross. Second day is short and easy

SUMMARY COMPARISON OF NORMAL AND VACAS VALLEY ROUTES

	Normal Route	Vacas Valley Route
Distance to basecamp	36km	47km
Distance to summit	Shorter	Longer, because of traverse around to the Normal Route
Difficulty	No rivers to cross. The walk to Plaza de Mulas is long and arduous. From there it is easier.	Two rivers to cross. Easier to basecamp, more difficult above.
Time	Shorter	At least one day longer each way
Water	None above basecamp	Streams up to Camp 2
Wind and cold	Sun does not reach camps until late morning	Sun hits camps early in the morning
Plants and animals	Relatively barren	Greener, more visible, all below Basecamp
Interest	Meet lots of people	Fewer people, more interesting countryside
Probability of reaching the summit	Lower (statistically)	Higher (statistically)
Cost	Lower	Two days' extra cost

TABLE OF CO-ORDINATES AND ELEVATIONS

Elevations in metres. Co-ordinates to UTM19S (Campo Inchauspe)

Location	Elevation	Eastings	Northings
Horcones	2535	411,860	6369,165
Confluencia	3420	409,385	6375,000
PLAZA DE MULAS	4365	400,890	6386,950
Camp Canada	5055	402,245	6387,460
Nido de Condores	5580	403,570	6388,285
Berlin	5850	404,320	6388,270
Punta de Vacas	2415	429,165	6364,765
Pampa de Leñas	2800	424,440	6375,800
Casa de Piedra	3200	421,465	6388,700
PLAZA ARGENTINA	4215	411,500	6387,460
Camp 1*	5000	408,405	6388,285
Camp Guanacos	5475	406,160	6389,130
Camp Cólera	5970	404,600	6388,355
Independencia	6400	404,843	6387,365
La Cueva	6675	404,805	6386,513
Aconcagua Summit	6962	405,200	6386,710

*Camp 1 is spread over a long, linear, sloping area

Climbers descending below Plaza Argentina

FOREWORD

Aconcagua is not merely a mountain to me. It is my life. As a mountain guide I have summitted Aconcagua too many times to recall.

Over three decades I have witnessed the number of climbers grow every year. In those three decades there has been more than a twelve-fold increase in numbers, and the increase continues.

We who serve these climbers must adapt to cater for the numbers. A guidebook such as this helps in this regard, and it improves our services to those who climb our mountain.

The degree of written material on Aconcagua when Jim's first edition was published was sparse. His map was one of the first detailed maps of the area in print. His focus was to produce a practical guide for the ordinary trekker, and he has succeeded.

It is up to us all to keep the mountain clean. Sadly cleanliness was neglected in the past, but the **Leave No Trace** policies are beginning to show results.

I welcome the new edition of Jim's book with its various updates and additions. I know it will sell as well as the earlier editions.

Sebastian Tetilla

Sebastian Tetilla
Mendoza

Trekking up the Relinchos Valley

PREFACE

This book is intended primarily for the many thousands who travel each year to climb the highest peak of the Americas – Aconcagua. The main concentration is the mountain itself. It is assumed that the traveller will fly into either Santiago or Mendoza, and remain in this general region before returning. The book is intended as a complete guide, so that it should not be necessary to bring supplementary books.

For every eight people who attempt the peak only two succeed, the majority failing due to altitude sickness or the weather, but also due to lack of preparation. A considerable section of the book is devoted to advice on acclimatisation and good preparations.

For those who prefer to acclimatise on mountains other than the primary goal, choices are offered near Mendoza (Vallecitos 5770m) and near Santiago (El Plomo 5430m). Many will want to get to the Aconcagua Provincial Park and acclimatise there, and treks are detailed near and within the park with this in mind.

The intriguing story of the aircraft flying from Mendoza to Santiago that crashed into a mountain and was swallowed in its glacier to re-emerge 50 years later is documented. A special wilderness trek within Tupungato Provincial Park to the site of the crashed plane is outlined.

The central regions of Chile and Argentina have much to offer besides the mountains of the Andes. For those who are forced to abandon the climb due to altitude or the weather, or who have time to spare, a range of other attractions are documented.

Information is included on the geology, plants and animals, customs and traditions, and even the language itself, to help you get the most out of your visit. The cities of Santiago and Mendoza have had a special relationship since their foundations. Their history, people, customs and architecture are fascinating.

Finally, if the book has succeeded in convincing you to go to Aconcagua you will find useful information in the appendices on places to stay and eat, shop and hire gear.

A NOTE ON THE THIRD EDITION

Over the past seven years there have been a number of changes that will impact on the climber. New topographical maps that are now available are listed. A detailed map, gridded for GPS, of Aconcagua from each basecamp to the summit has been added. A full list of camps with their GPS coordinates is included. Climbing Cerro Bonete (5004m) from Plaza de Mulas has been added. On the Vacas Valley Route trekking companies now tend to camp at Camp Guanacos and Camp Cólera rather than Camp 2 and Camp 3, respectively. Global warming has reduced the *penitentes* in height and in number. High inflation and the downward slide of the peso continues to affect costs in Argentina, with the exchange rate in 2017 at 16 to the dollar.

The view to the south face of Aconcagua over the lake at Horcones

INTRODUCTION

Suspension bridge over Rio Horcones on the Normal Route

The mountain of Aconcagua is the highest peak in the world outside of the Himalayas and the mountains of eastern Asia. It is the highest of the seven summits after Everest, and offers the climber the best value in terms of altitude gained for effort expended.

The purist might contend that climbing in double plastic boots, with crampons and an ice axe, in temperatures of -20°C, can hardly be classified as a 'trek'. Nevertheless, Aconcagua requires not much technical expertise, and provides valuable high-altitude experience.

Over the recent past the pursuit of climbing and hill walking has attracted more and more enthusiasts. While travel to far-off places has become more popular and easier to arrange, mountain guides clog the internet with advertisements of their adventure holidays. And for those who tire of the commonplace, goals such as Kilimanjaro, Island Peak and Aconcagua are there to provide the adventure.

Aconcagua is seen as an essential stepping-stone for those with eyes on the big prize – Everest. However, the serious alpinist will have to rub shoulders with the adventurous trekker. Like any mountain, there are numerous routes up Aconcagua.

While the majority are categorised as extremely difficult, two routes are available that require minimal technical expertise, and it is these routes that are described in detail in this guidebook.

The area of South America in which Aconcagua is situated is quite civilised, transport is good, and there is an established infrastructure for mountain access. There are no nasties in the region, such as snakes, mosquitoes or wild cats; the people are friendly; food is great; and language is not a particular barrier. The region also has many other attractions, such as the vineyards of Chile and Mendoza, white water rafting, the beach at Viña del Mar, rodeos and numerous other scenic and cultural items of interest.

However, it is not all a bed of roses. Aconcagua is bleak and harsh. The winds can be unrelenting, and the temperatures severe. The incidence of failure due to altitude sickness and weather is particularly high. Many climbers arrive unprepared for the cold and the altitude, so repeat visits are common. Chile and Argentina are developing countries, and costs are comparable to the costs in Europe and North America.

THE MOUNTAIN IN CONTEXT

There are no less than 164 peaks in Eastern Asia in the Himalayas, Karakoram, Hindu Kush, Tian Shan, Daxue Shan and Kunlun that have greater altitudes than Aconcagua. In the Americas, however, Aconcagua tops a list of 43 peaks, all in South America, ahead of Denali (McKinley).

Alpinists consider Aconcagua to be much more difficult than a large proportion of its Asian cousins. They attribute this to its harsh environment, unpredictable weather, the dreaded Canaleta scree slope that must be overcome at 6700m and its long distance to basecamp. The relative distance of Aconcagua from the equator, compared to those in East

THE HIGHEST MOUNTAINS OF THE SEVEN CONTINENTS

Continent	Mountain	Height
Asia	Everest	8850m/29,035ft
South America	Aconcagua	6962m/22,841ft
North America	Denali	6194m/20,320ft
Africa	Kilimanjaro	5895m/19,341ft
Europe	Elbrus	5642m/18,510ft
Antarctica	Vinson Massif	4897m/16,066ft
Oceania	Puncak Jaya	4884m/16,023ft

THE HIGHEST PEAKS OF THE AMERICAS		
	Height	Country
1 Aconcagua	6962m	Argentina
2 Ojos del Salado	6891m	Argentina–Chile
3 Pissis	6792m	Argentina
4 Huascarán	6768m	Peru
5 Bonéte	6759m	Argentina
6 Tres Cruces	6758m	Argentina–Chile
7 Llullaillaco	6723m	Argentina–Chile
8 Mercedario	6720m	Argentina
9 Cazadero	6658m	Argentina
10 Incahuasi	6638m	Argentina–Chile
11 Yerupajá	6634m	Peru
12 Tupungato	6565m	Argentina–Chile

Asia, is considered to be a factor in terms of weather and altitude. The further you travel from the equator, the thinner is the earth's atmosphere.

TWO TREKKING ROUTES

Every mountain has a diversity of routes to the summit, and Aconcagua is no exception. This guidebook

Sign at Plaza Argentina

covers the two most popular, non-technical ascents, with a brief reference to the more challenging direct route up the Polish Glacier.

More than 60 per cent of all climbers take the **Normal Route** (Ruta Normale). This is also known as the Horcones Valley Route. The approach is from the south, 36km over a rough river valley to basecamp at Plaza de Mulas. From Plaza de Mulas the route swings around to the east, over steep ground, eventually turning directly south to the summit.

The second popular trekking route is known as the **Vacas Valley Route**, but is also commonly known as the Polish Glacier Route, or even the False Polish Glacier Route. It is 47km from the road head to basecamp at Plaza Argentina. Initially the direction is, like the Normal Route, due north for 31km, then a left turn to the west, and a further 16km up the Relinchos River valley.

Both routes join high up the mountain, at Camp Cólera (5970m), a relatively new campsite with an emergency refuge in it.

Via the Normal Route the summit will be visible for much of the journey to basecamp, whereas on the Vacas Valley Route it only comes into view when you reach the left-hand turn after 31km. The average time (subject to acclimatisation) to the summit and back to the road head is 12 days via the Normal Route and 14 days on the Vacas Valley Route. The Vacas Valley Route is less crowded and more picturesque. Consequently there is more bird life and even the possibility of seeing some wild guanacos (a type of llama).

The Vacas Valley Route is tougher and longer than the Normal Route. However, for those not acclimatised, this pays dividends when you are better prepared for summit day. Acclimatisation on another mountain, such as at Vallecitos or El Plomo, then climbing via the Normal Route, is a good option.

What is known as the 360-degree expedition has become very popular: climb the mountain via the Vacas Valley and then descend via Plaza de Mulas.

LOCATION

Aconcagua is entirely within the Republic of Argentina, very close to the border with Chile. Halfway south to the middle of Chile and below the Tropic of Capricorn, it is in the province of Mendoza and the department of Las Heras.

The Aconcagua Provincial Park is immediately off the main road that links the cities of Mendoza in Argentina and Santiago in Chile. Of the 13 passes over the Andes between the two countries this is one of only two paved roads. On the southern side of the road another of Mendoza's provincial parks – The Tupungato Provincial Park – begins.

The nearest village on the main road is Puente del Inca, which is 15km inside the Argentina/Chile border, 186km from Mendoza and 169km from Santiago. Between the starting points of the two trekking routes lies Los Penitentes, a ski resort in the winter, deserted in the spring and autumn, with a cable car (closed during the summer) up to the mountains.

GEOLOGY

Charles Darwin was the first explorer to examine the geology of the high Andes. His 1835 sketch of the Puente del Inca rock formation remains a classic. The German geologist Walter Schiller, however, is recognised as the father of Andean geology, perhaps only surpassed in recent times by Victor Ramos.

The geological deposits of Aconcagua can be divided into three periods:

- the base sedimentary rocks
- the higher volcanic rocks, and
- the glacial and alluvial deposits

The base sedimentary rocks range in age from the Carboniferous, through the Permian, Triassic, Jurassic into the Cretaceous period. So they are approximately 100 to 300 million years old. The base rocks under the Vacas Valley are the oldest rocks. These Carboniferous slates can be seen on the high ground east of Puente del Inca, and above Los Penitentes.

The Permian ignimbritic and pyroclastic rocks that form the sides of the Vacas Valley are the second oldest. Up at the south face of Aconcagua, near Plaza Francia, red Jurassic and early Cretaceous limestones are visible at the western base. On the walk in to Confluencia a grey limestone boulder field will be passed. These boulders have come

The mix of sedimentary and volcanic rocks of Cerro Almacenes above Confluencia

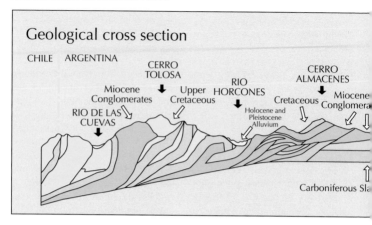

Geological cross section

CHILE   ARGENTINA

CERRO
TOLOSA

Miocene   ↓   Upper   RIO
Conglomerates   Cretaceous   HORCONES   ↓

RIO DE LAS ↘
CUEVAS

Holocene and
Pleistocene
Alluvium

CERRO
ALMACENES
↓   Miocene
Cretaceous   Conglomera

Carboniferous Sl

down from a Jurassic formation high on the mountain.

Tectonic plate movements have lifted up and twisted these rocks. Fault lines and dramatic folds are common. Volcanic activity accompanied the tectonic plate movements, so that these older deposits support extensive masses of volcanic lavas and ashes of more recent date.

The convergence of the oceanic plate and the South American plate, estimated at 90 to 100mm per annum, has resulted in a number of major earthquakes in the region, notably one in 1861 which destroyed Mendoza, and even one as recent as 1985 with an epicentre in Valparaiso.

Metamorphic heat has transformed some of the sedimentary rocks. Great mountains of trachyte rise from the sedimentary base. In his 1884 treatise *Der Vulkan Aconcagua*, the German naturalist and climber Paul

Gussfeldt postulated that there likely was once a crater on the south summit.

The predominant rock found on Aconcagua is a grey rock with black particles. It is not unlike sandstone, but has been positively identified as a volcanic Andesite. This same rock outcrops on the summit and can be seen on many of the scree slopes. Above the Berlin camp, below Rocas Blancas, on the west and north sides, there are areas of thermal clay. These are yellowish in colour and contain sulphur. This suggests that Aconcagua is an extinct volcano or an uplifted volcano, perched on top of a sedimentary base.

The river valleys south of the mountain contain deep deposits of gravel from four periods of glaciation and from natural erosion. Ice and frost on the mountain account for much of this erosion. In the Horcones valley these glacial and alluvial deposits are up to 5m deep, cut through by the

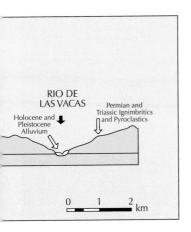

RIO DE
LAS VACAS

Holocene and
Pleistocene
Alluvium

Permian and
Triassic Ignimbritics
and Pyroclastics

0   1   2
km

river. The Horcones and Vacas rivers have a high discharge and flow very fast in the summer season, as the snow and ice above melts. The water is dark red in colour, as it conveys its load of suspended solids down to deposit it in the valleys below.

TOPOGRAPHY

The central Andes is divided into four north–south *cordilleras*. Immediately west of Mendoza is the relatively low **Precordillera**. This is the mountain range that blocks a view of the high peaks from the city. Beyond it to the west is the **Frontal Cordillera** that includes peaks such as Vallecitos (5770m) and El Plata (6300m). The **Principal Cordillera** includes Aconcagua (6962m), Tupungato (6550m) and El Plomo (5430m). Finally, west of Santiago is the **Coastal Cordillera** that has mountains such as La Campana (1880m) and Roble Alto (2198m).

From the Vallecitos area there is a mountain range that stretches across in a northeast–southwest direction from the Frontal Cordillera towards Tupungato in the Principal Cordillera. This range is known as Cordón del Plata. It includes El Plata (6300m) and Vallecitos (5770m).

The climbing history of Aconcagua documents many attempts at finding a route to the summit, via the various valleys, over glaciers, etc. This provides some insight into the difficult terrain in the area. There are no

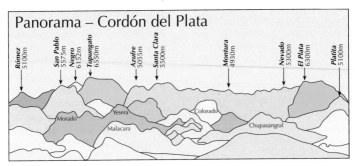

Panorama – Cordón del Plata

Rómez 5100m · San Pablo 5575m · Negro 6152m · Tupungato 6550m · Azufre 5055m · Santa Clara 5500m · Montura 4930m · Nevado 5300m · El Plata 6300m · Platita 5100m

Morado · Yesera · Malacara · Colorado · Chupasangral

The penitentes above Plaza Argentina

fewer than 13 peaks with an altitude of more than 5000m that encircle Aconcagua.

The jagged appearances of the mountains at high-level contrast with the smooth river valleys below. Sharp mountain features mellow into scree slopes that sweep down to the rivers. Landslides are common in these valleys.

There are five main glaciers in the Aconcagua area. The most significant for the climber is the Polish Glacier that covers the eastern side of the mountain. However, the Horcones Inferior Glacier, which swings around from behind the Mirador mountain (directly south of Aconcagua) to run down to within a few kilometres of the campsite of Confluencia, is much bigger. This glacier, which is hardly

recognizable from the air because it is covered in scree, is up to 20 metres in depth. A slowly moving mass of ice, it groans and squeaks as it slides down the valley.

Minor glaciers abound on Aconcagua. Some, like the Horcones Inferior Glacier, are covered in rocks and scree, tens of metres thick, slowly moving down the valleys. Others are white and covered with penitentes.

The penitentes of Aconcagua are a particular feature of the region. These ice spikes can be as low as a few centimetres or as high as four metres. Caused by the very cold winds on the mountain, the penitentes are set out in a linear pattern, generally with approximately half a metre between spikes. Wonderful to photograph, particularly when they are white, these penitentes present a formidable barrier to the climber.

The Horcones Valley approach has a pleasant area near the road head that provides a 'picture postcard' view of the mountain. With the harsh white outline of the peak in the background Laguna Horcones is a green, lush picnic point 3km from the road.

Sightseers will often drive in off the main highway, away from the noise of the busy traffic to the tranquillity of the water's edge.

MAPS AND CO-ORDINATES

Until 2005 there were no maps of Aconcagua National Park (except the map in the first edition of this book). In 2005–2006 two topographical maps were issued: one at 1:40,000; the other at 1:50,000. Neither are GPS user-friendly. One is gridded in degrees and minutes, the other uses the wrong UTM (metric) zone. The 1:50,000 has all of the campsite co-ordinates, but they are in degrees, minutes and seconds. It has the wrong location of the permit office in its street map of Mendoza (see also 'Maps, guides and further reading' in Appendix A).

The new map in this book (Routes to the Summit) is properly gridded in metric and is compatible with any GPS.

In your GPS:
- Set the Position Format to UTM UPS
- Set the Map Datum to Campo Inchspe

When you operate your GPS you will see that the location has the prefix 19H. This is the UTM zone that covers Aconcagua. Campo Inchspe is the geodetic datum suitable for Argentina.

The coordinates to this format and datum of all of the campsites, starting points and landmarks are listed in a the Table of co-ordinates and elevations in Part 1.

WILDLIFE

During the summer low growing cactus and other wildflowers provide minimal ground cover in as far as Confluencia on the Horcones Valley route and as far as Plaza Argentina on the Vacas Valley Route. Nasturtiums in large yellow clusters and whitish/pink calandrinia will be plentiful in the spring and early summer. In

The beautiful nasturtium Tropaeolum polyphyllum, *treasured in Europe, is a wildflower native to this region*

November the viola is just beginning to show flower at its rims.

There are small areas of grass, more frequent in the Vacas Valley, and, yes, it is most likely that you will see cows grazing on this grass in the Vacas Valley (Valley of Cows).

There is a distinct probability that, on a trek to the summit, you will not see a single live animal, not even a rodent, but you will see an abundance of small birds, particularly on the Vacas Valley Route. Larger birds are rare and there are few of any size above the basecamps. Small lizards will often be seen, scurrying in the rocks in the Vacas Valley below Pampa de Leñas.

The condor of South America is a very large bird that hovers in the sky. Other birds of prey, *carancho andino*, of the same features as condors, but with a degree of white on the wings and rear body, similarly hover, are much smaller and are often mistaken for condors. A condor has a wingspan of more than 3 metres, and the ends of its wings have a band of silver feathers and are distinctly serrated. In between the condor and the carancho in size is the *jote cabeza negra* (or, if it has a red head, *jote cabeza roja*). This is also a black vulture that hovers, but has no white feathers.

The grey-hooded sierra finch is a common visitor to the lower camps. Scraps of food will entice them into photo range and some may even be cheeky enough to enter the mess tents at basecamp. A bird that will be heard though seldom seen is the *perdicita* (*Perdix perdix*), which is similar to the European partridge. It is the same size as a thrush and has the same mottled wings, but its head is grey and its legs orange. The perdicita's call is similar to a pump that needs oil. Perdicitas are very common at Pampa de Leñas and Confluencia.

On the El Plomo trek there will be many birds at Piedra Numerada, including the noisy perdicita. The brown birds with grey breasts and a golden scalp are *dormilonas fraile*.

The red fox, hares and guanacos are the only animals you have a chance of seeing, the guanaco only in the Vacas Valley. The red fox of

The zorro, or red fox

Guanaco

the Andes, *Dusicyon culpaeus*, is the same size as a domestic dog. Its red fur is generally grey-white on its back. The fox will seldom be seen during the daytime, but may wander around the lower campsites at night, searching for scraps. Beware: it can transmit rabies.

Guanacos, *Llama guanicoe*, are relatives of, and similar to, the *vicuñas* further north, and also to the common South American domesticated llama. They have a curled yellow fur with a white belly. Roaming in small herds, they are very nervous animals that avoid human presence. Guanacos are amazingly agile. Upon detecting potential predators they will run high into the hills. The herd will generally consist of several females and their young and one dominant male. They make high-pitched calls, and their droppings are similar to those of sheep.

Ancient history

The ancient history of southern Chile and Argentina is not well documented. Humans are thought to have crossed from North to South America approximately 15,000 years ago, reaching down as far as Tierra del Fuego some 10,000 years later.

Tribes such as the Mapuche, Aymaras and later the Wari are believed to have been early inhabitants of Chile before the Incas. The Mapuche people lived south of Santiago and dominated most of Argentina.

The Incas, the Mapuche and the Huarpe

From sometime in the later part of the 15th century to the middle of the 16th century the Incas took control of northern Chile, but were repelled from Argentina by the Mapuche in the south and the Huarpes in the Mendoza area.

There is evidence that the Incas held the mountains in high regard, that they climbed them and used the mountains to offer sacrifices to their gods. In 1947, a guanaco was discovered between the north and south ridge of Aconcagua and it was considered that the guanaco was brought there as a sacrifice. Since then, the ridge has been known as Cresta del Guanaco.

Mummies have been uncovered on this and other peaks. On the

Cerro El Plomo
(5,400 m, Chile central)

Momia Cerro Aconcagua
(cambiada de Piramide, 5,300 m,
NW de Mendoza, Argentina)

Momia Cerro El Toro
(6,160 m, NW de San Juan, Argentina)

Reconstrucción de la vestimenta
de una mujer joven, semejante
a una tumba del Nevado de Quehuar
Perú. (5800 m.)

*Representation of the Aconcagua
mummy at the Museo Cornelio
Moyano, Mendoza*

nearby peak of Cerro Piramidal, for
instance, the mummified remains of
a young girl were discovered. Another
was unearthed on top of the 6723m
mountain of Llullaillaco. On the summit of El Plomo, at 5430m, overlooking the city of Santiago, there is an
Incan altar and a burial site where the
mummified remains of a child were
discovered in 1954.

In Mendoza's Parque General
San Martin there is a small natural
history museum, Museo Cornelio
Moyano. Housed in the museum
until relatively recently (now in the
Criant nearby) were the remains of
the mummy found at 5300m on the
southwestern side of Aconcagua.

Advent of the Spanish Conquistadors
The Spanish conquests of the Incas
by Pizarro in the middle of the 16th
century were to change the history
of the entire western side of South
America. In 1520 Magellan had discovered the straits that allowed trade
between Spain and Asia. Spanish
expeditions from the north eventually
led to the invasion by Valdivia, the
great Spanish general, who founded
the city of Santiago.

The first contact between the
Spanish and the Huarpas was in 1551,
when an exploratory expedition was
sent over the Andes. Ten years later,
in 1561 the then captain general of
Santiago, General Mendoza, sent
his captain, Pedro de Castillo, with
a major force over the Andes where
the city of Mendoza was founded,
and called after him. Thus Mendoza
became a province of Santiago,
despite the enormous obstacle of the
Andes in between. Cultural and commercial ties between the two cities
that developed in the 16th century
remain today.

Decades of conflict followed
with the Mapuche. General Valdivia
himself was killed by them in 1553.
Then, in 1641, a treaty was reached
leaving them autonomous below the
River Biobio. Only as late at the 19th
century did the Mapuche integrate to
become part of Chile.

Spanish colonial rule followed in both countries until the early part of the 19th century, when Napoleon invaded Spain. The consequent uncertainty ended with Chile declaring independence in 1810, and Argentina following in 1816. It was not until 1818, however, that the great heroes of Chile, José de San Martin and Bernardo O'Higgins, formally created the new nation, following the final defeat of the Royalists.

Mendoza suffered a severe earthquake in 1861. With the epicentre in the heart of the city the devastation was enormous, and thousands were killed. Relief for the homeless came from around the globe and helped to have the city rebuilt.

An earthquake on the Chilean side accounted for 3,882 deaths in 1906, and Chile's worst in 1939 resulted in 28,000 deaths.

Recent history

Both countries have had colourful recent pasts. Chile's wealth was initially built on copper, silver and nitrates while Argentina's economy was largely centred on cattle and sheep. Nowadays wine production is a relatively new source of wealth for both countries, Chile producing more than Argentina. It is interesting to note that Aconcagua is one of the five demarcated wine regions of Chile. Chile produces and exports fruit, and among its natural resources copper is significant.

The production of maize, soya and other crops continues to be significant for Argentina, and, of course, Argentinean beef has a world reputation. Garlic is an important Mendocino product. South of Mendoza there are a number of small oil wells. Natural gas fuels much of the heating for the towns of Chilean Patagonia.

Water from the Andes provides irrigation for vineyards and cultivation on both sides of the mountains. It provides drinking water, and the dam at Potrerillos provides electricity. Similarly a dam on the Rio Colorado provides electricity on the Chilean side.

Chile courted socialism, in 1886 with president Balmaceda, in 1920 with president Palma, and finally in 1970 with Salvador Allende. A workers' supported military coup brought Juan Peron to power in Argentina in 1946. Military rule continued until President Galtieri took on the British in his ill-fated invasion of the Falklands in 1982.

In 1985 Mendoza was rocked by another earthquake, but the damage to the relatively new low-rise buildings was not significant. Valparaiso was the epicentre of Chile's most recent earthquakes in 1971 and 1985.

Chile has a population of 17 million, of which the Mapuche account for nearly 1 million. The majority of the population is *mestizo*, which is a mix of Hispanic and Indian. By contrast the vast majority of Argentina's 36

Tupungato in the background over the Norton vineyard

million people are of European decent. Italy was the origin of many original Mendocinos. Their attachment to their Italian ancestors is marked by a major festival in March every year, centred around Plaza Italia.

The people who live and work in the mountain region, on either side of the border, have distinctive Indo-European features.

Chile suffered under the regime that followed Allende and many fled the country. Since the 1990s, there has been a gradual return of these exiles, many from Spain. The returning exiles brought back with them new ideas that sparked a revitalisation of the culture of Chile. This is most clearly seen in its modern architecture. In Valparaiso there is a school of architecture that has achieved world standing.

Of Chile's current domestic problems the claim by the Mapuche for their land rights has never gone away. The Mapuche contend that many millions of hectares of traditional Mapuche lands was taken by the government and sold. A similar, though not as contentious, problem with the Mapuches exists over the border in Argentina where Mapuche demonstrators are squatting at the United Colours of Benneton sheep farm.

In the countryside around Mendoza and Tupungato there are many Bolivian migrant workers who toil in the sun cultivating vegetables. The Mendocinos, it has to be said, tend to look down on the Bolivians.

The 2015 United Nations' Human Development Index (which includes life expectancy, education and income per capita) ranked Argentina in 40th place and Chile in 42nd place, both higher than any other South American country. The centres of cities such as Buenos Aires and Santiago display affluence but there is deep poverty in the countryside, particularly in Chile.

The collapse of the Argentinean economy in 2001/2002 was a turning point for this once great nation.

Inflation during that year reached 300 per cent, unemployment soared, and political unrest was rife. Within a brief two years Argentinean society had tumbled from its perch as the most affluent in South America to one that resembled its poorer northern neighbours. The economy has since steadied, and confidence is gradually being restored. But the cities show distinct signs of neglect: there is no money for infrastructural maintenance; there are holes in the pavements; roads needing surfacing; drainage channels are collapsing; and municipal buildings are neglected.

Because of Argentina's high inflation and tax regime consumer goods in Chile are much cheaper than in Argentina. Border smuggling is the inevitable consequence.

Argentinean–Chilean relationships

These neighbours have been close to war on a number of occasions, all related to border disputes. Queen Victoria arbitrated between then in 1902, and Queen Elizabeth in 1977. It was not until the 1990s that the presidents of both countries made a lasting peace.

The enormous statue on the border, *Cristo Redentor* (Christ the Redeemer), was erected by both countries as a sign of peace after the 1902 treaty. The area of the statue, on the original old road, was a particular point of dispute, so that to erect it on the agreed border was to mark its significance. The inscription on its plaque reads: 'These mountains will fall before the peace between our countries is broken.'

Santiago's modern architecture

Market stall at Puenta del Inca

Although the border has been the main source of dispute there has always been a good relationship between the cities of Santiago and Mendoza. The proximity of Mendoza to Santiago, rather than to its national capital, Buenos Aires, and the excellent road and air connections, are undoubtedly factors in this relationship. The Spanish that is spoken in Mendoza is more akin to Chilean Spanish than to Argentinean Spanish and a trip to the seaside, for Mendocinos, has always been via Santiago to Viña del Mar.

CLIMBING HISTORY

The mountain pass over the Andes to the south of Aconcagua, now Route 7 from Santiago to Mendoza, was an ancient Inca trail, and the mountain is clearly visible from the pass. This

pass was used by José de San Martin and Bernardo O'Higgins to bring the 'Great Army of the Andes' down into Chile to defeat the Spanish in 1818.

Charles Darwin visited the region in 1835, and is reputed to have experienced earth tremors during his excursion ashore from the *Beagle*. Paul Gussfeldt, a German climber and naturalist, made an unsuccessful attempt at the summit in 1883.

In late 1896 the Englishman, Edward Fitzgerald, led a serious expedition. In his team were the Swiss climber, Matthias Zurbriggen, and another English climber Stuart Vines.

They set off from the mountain pass up the Vacas Valley, decided this was an impossible route, and returned to try the Lower Horcones Valley. Concluding that the south face was too difficult they returned to Confluencia and proceeded up the Normal Route.

After many weeks on the mountain Matthias Zurbriggen arrived on the summit on 14 January 1897. A month later Vines and an Italian porter named Nicola Lanti summitted. Fitzgerald himself unfortunately never made it due to altitude sickness. He did, however, write a detailed account of his expedition, listing the conditions he encountered, the plants and animals he had identified. This treatise remains today as an important document, not only in relation to Aconcagua, but also to the early studies of the Andes.

In March 1934 four Polish climbers, Konstanty Narkievicz-Jodko, Stefan Osiecki, Wiktor Ostrowski and Stefan Daszynski, ascended via the Polish Glacier. Part of a six-man party, they had ascended via the Vacas and Relinchos valleys. Severe weather had kept the party pinned on the glacier at 6300m, until they could make the decisive thrust to the summit. The Polish Glacier is named after them.

A French team travelled up the Lower Horcones Valley in 1954, and established a campsite (now known as Plaza Francia) under the south face. One month later six of the team reached the summit. It was late in the evening and they descended via the Normal Route. However, they were lucky to be picked up by other climbers, and they suffered severe frostbite.

The Polish Glacier – the Vacas Valley route now avoids the glacier entirely

The Argentinean army controlled the area until 1980, imposing many restrictions. In 1983 the area was declared a provincial park, opening the way to its popularity. Argentina has 22 national parks, yet, although Aconcagua attracts many thousands of visitors every year, it has not yet been elevated to national park status.

During the first open season in 1983, 356 people climbed the mountain. In the 2002/2003 season this had risen to almost 6000 (3800 climbers and 2132 low level trekkers), more than a ten-fold increase; and in 2007 the figure was 7500. The numbers peaked at 7000 in 2009 when the summit cost was 1500 pesos (€435). When the Mendoza government began to lift the cost significantly higher than the rate of inflation, and

with the world recession, the numbers began to drop, so that by 2012 the entrants were only 5500. Since then the government has ceased to publish statistics, presumably embarrassed by the drop-off.

These permit fees are very high. Compare the 2017 rate of $945 to Kilimanjaro where the cost is a mere $70, or to Denali at $365. There is no fee to enter and climb Tupungato 6565m in Tupungato National Park across the road. Nor is there a fee for Cerro de La Plata 6100m.

As early as 1990 the government decided on a programme of cleaning and maintenance. Mules were taken as high as Independencia to remove rubbish. Strict procedures were adopted to keep the mountain clean, with refuse sacks being issued

Expedition en route to Plaza de Mulas

The hotel at Plaza de Mulas has been closed for six years

to all climbers. These restrictions on waste have recently been further reinforced. It is only permissible now to camp in the designated campsites, and climbers above the lower camps must contract with a service provider to accept and dispose of human faeces.

In 1992 the hotel was constructed near Plaza de Mulas (it has not been used now for many years). The worrying incidences of rock fall, particularly one that destroyed 10 tents, forced the authorities to move Plaza des Mulas in 1997. Confluencia was also moved in 1999 to control pollution.

There are various recordings of ascents and descents over the years. The fastest ascent, from Plaza de Mulas to the summit, has steadily decreased from 9 hours in 1987 to 3 hours 40 minutes in 2000. The fastest descent was by a paraglider in 1985 when A. Steves of the French Air Force came down in 25 minutes. In 1991 and 1992 records were further set for an ascent and descent in one day via the normal route and the Polish Glacier route.

Of more interest to normal trekkers is the shortest time from the main road at Horcones up to the summit and back, and this was set by Ecuadorian Karl Egloff in 2015 at an amazing 11 hours 52 minutes.

TREKKER/CLIMBER PROFILES

A wide range of people come to climb Aconcagua. In general, approximately 11–18 per cent are female. Of the low level trekkers the percentage of

*Plaza de Mulas
under snow*

females increases to 35 per cent. 25 per cent of climbers and 60 per cent of trekkers are Argentineans. The next country with the largest numbers is the United States, followed by Germany, Spain, France and the United Kingdom. Climbers from Canada frequent the mountain more than those from Chile, Switzerland and Japan.

A recent new regulation restricts minors on climbing. No person under 14 may go any higher than 3100m. A minor over 14, but under the age of consent, requires the written permission of both of his parents, witnessed by a notary. If the minor is climbing with one of the parents, then the written permission of the other, again notary witnessed, is required. The forms for such consents may be downloaded from the Mendoza government website.

The age of consent in Argentina is 21; thus, if you are an Argentinean aged 20 you may not obtain a permission to climb without these forms.

The weather on Aconcagua

The most predictable aspect of the weather on Aconcagua is its unpredictability. During the summer months it will generally be very windy all the time. Out of the wind, down in the valleys, the temperature will be as high as 27°C at midday and as low as 3°C at midnight. At top camp the temperature will fall to at least -15°C at night, possibly as low as -30°C. In the middle of the day on the summit the temperature could range from as low as -35°C to as high as 10°C.

During the summer on the mountain it will be cold in the morning until the sun shines. The welcome solar heat always hits Plaza Argentina earlier than Plaza de Mulas. After 6pm sunset will fast descend and the temperature will drop sharply within a short period.

An important feature of the weather on Aconcagua is the wind chill factor. When the wind is particularly strong and cold this factor can have the effect of lowering the temperature, from the leeward side to the wind side, by as much as 15°C.

The region is subject to El Niño, a summer phenomenon in the southern hemisphere that can dramatically alter the weather. The cold Antarctic waters that flow northwards along the South American coast are deflected to the west. Warmer seas, with more evaporation mean heavy rain. El Niño is as likely to influence dry weather as it is wet weather, and there have been periods of very wet weather and extreme drought.

The predominant winds in the central Andes come from the west or the southwest. As they rise over the mountains their velocity increases. In summer their precipitation is rarely in the form of rain, usually snow. During the day, therefore, winds whip through the valleys. At night ice-cold winds come down from the mountaintops.

Aconcagua itself has its own microclimate. The weather can be pleasant in the central Andes while

A storm over Aconcagua contrasts with tranquillity at Horcones

A mule train en route out of Confluencia

a storm is raging up on Aconcagua. Electric storms are not uncommon during the summer. Occasionally the weather will produce a mushroom of cloud over the summit, with severe winds and driving snow.

Weather watching is a particular expertise of the local guides, and much of their conversations revolve around this topic. Winds from the south are a sign of good weather, those from the north or the west are not. The guides will know what the normal barometric pressure is at each campsite and they will be alerted by changes in the barometer.

On all of the Andean peaks the daily pattern tends to an early clearance of cloud that may provide clear weather until midday. In the early afternoon the tendency is for the clouds to appear, engulfing the

summit by mid to late afternoon, then clearing again as night falls. Summiting at midday is therefore a good plan.

During the 2001/2002 season in the period from 24 December to 30 December, the wind blew down the Horcones valley from the north. A blizzard greeted new arrivals at Plaza de Mulas on 1 January. Many of them had left Confluencia in T-shirts and shorts, and were caught unawares. Meanwhile, up on the mountain there were no successful summits for 5 days, and only nine successful attempts in the succeeding 2 days. Hundreds of climbers went home disappointed. Determined climbers descended to recover, recalling six nights of -26°C.

By 2009 global warming had reduced the volume of snow on the mountain and curtailed the extent of glaciers and penitentes. Now, eight years later, it is becoming a rarity to have snow in the summer.

In early January 2003 there was snow on the summit, and the Canaleta was relatively easy to climb with crampons. Within a few days the snow was gone and the Canaleta scree had returned to its loose nature. The winds whipped up, gusting to over 100km/hour. The wind chill reduced temperatures by 15°C. The severe winds only lasted a few days. When they abated, the weather was ideal for climbing, and the temperature on the summit was in the mid teens Centigrade.

In January 2009 frozen snow on the Canaleta made climbing it easy. Conversely, underfoot conditions on the Polish Glacier were poor. A layer of soft snow covered the ice, so that securing a foothold was often difficult. Tragically these conditions are blamed for the loss of life of three people, all within days of each other in early January 2009.

During the 2016/2017 season winds of more than 100km/hr ensured that climbers were confined to the basecamps from Christmas to the New Year.

Climate in Santiago/Mendoza

During the summer it will generally be a little warmer and more humid in Mendoza than across the mountains in Santiago. Whereas there will be virtually no chance of rain during the Santiago summer, in Mendoza the summer season is not only the warm season, but also the wet season. A monthly summer rainfall of only 20mm to 30mm is nevertheless extremely small. Santiago has more than double Mendoza's rainfall, but it all falls during the winter.

WHEN TO GO

The climbing season on Aconcagua is from mid November to mid March, during the South American summer. In mid November it is springtime in South America, but the snow on the Andes is deep, and the weather unpredictable. The various camps are being set up and the *arrieros* are only coming up from the lowlands. December and January is high season, when 80 per cent of climbers come. The weather is best from mid December to early February. By mid March the summer has ended and those who serve the climbers are packing up for another year. Once again the incidences of storms in the Andes increase.

At the height of the season the basecamps are crowded, mules are nearly all pre-booked, accommodation at Los Penitentes and Puente del Inca is full, the cost of a permit is high, and an additional premium is added to almost everything. On the Normal Route there are many climbers vying for clean snow to melt, and sanitation suffers.

To climb outside of the designated climbing season nevertheless requires a permit. In order to discourage

TEMPERATURES AND RAINFALL IN SANTIAGO AND MENDOZA

Month	Max/Min Temp (°C)		Monthly rainfall (mm)	
	Santiago	Mendoza	Santiago	Mendoza
December	28/11	30/15	5	20
January	29/12	32/16	3	29
February	29/12	30/15	3	33
March	27/10	27/13	5	28
April	23/8	23/8	13	13
May	18/6	18/7	64	10
June	14/4	14/3	84	9
July	15/3	14/2	76	8
August	17/4	17/4	56	5
September	19/6	19/7	31	13
October	21/8	21/10	15	17
November	22/9	27/11	8	18

The permit office in Mendoza

PEAK TREKKING TIMES

Month	Week	% of trekkers
November	3	1.0
	4	2.3
December	1	4.0
	2	5.8
	3	10.0
	4	12.6
January	1	14.0
	2	13.0
	3	11.1
	4	8.2
February	1	9.1
	2	5.0
	3	2.3
	4	1.0
March	1	0.5
	2	0.1

climbers when there is no emergency rescue, no ranger control and no services on the mountain, the authorities impose a higher than normal rate.

The best balance of avoiding the crowds and advantageous weather is the two weeks before Christmas, or the last week in January and the first week in February. There is a surge of people who want to celebrate Christmas then leave for the climb. A review of the statistics shows, for some strange reason, a dip in the numbers who arrive in the last week in January.

The table shows the official figures of trekkers on the mountain, calculated by taking an average over many

seasons. The variation from year to year does not seem to significantly change.

Mendoza is very busy in late February and early March with wine harvesting. The first week in March is the great wine festival, when the city is filled with visitors. Accommodation will be difficult to procure, and many of those working on Aconcagua may have returned to the lowlands to help with the harvest and join in the festivities. However, if accommodation is secure, the carnival atmosphere can be an exhilarating way to finish an expedition.

GETTING THERE

The Aconcagua roadhead lies roughly midway along the main road from Mendoza to Santiago. However, since you have to obtain a permit in person at Mendoza, it follows that this city is the required starting point.

International flights do not land in Mendoza. The nearest international airport is Santiago, 35 minutes away by plane, or Buenos Aires, 1½ hours away. Bear in mind that the domestic airport in Buenos Aires is 40km from the international airport, so you will need to factor in the cost, time and headache of transferring between airports.

The following airlines operate into Chile and Argentina:
• Latam
• Iberia
• American Airlines
• Alitalia

- Qantas
- Cathay Pacific
- Luftansa
- British Airways

It pays to take some time in planning the flights, and examining cost alternatives. An experienced global travel agent can reduce your flight costs by anything up to one-third. Give due attention to the baggage allowance; with all the gear, you can expect to be carrying over 25kg. Iberia's allowance is 23kg, whereas British Airways allows 46kg. Airline check-ins in Europe and North America are more lenient than those in South America, so you may get a nasty surprise if your luggage is a few kilograms overweight.

Cabin air filtration on long-haul flights differs from airline to airline. The easiest place to pick up an infection is on an air flight. The altitude has a way of seeking out any minor ailments and exacerbating them. Thus, a mild chest infection can rise to pneumonia quite easily on the mountain. In general, the European and American airlines have better air filtration than the South American ones.

São Paulo, in Brazil, is a common stopover en route from Europe. The flight from São Paulo or Madrid to Santiago circles around Aconcagua before descending to land. The view from the aeroplane can be quite spectacular – so try to get a seat on the right-hand side of the plane. Flying from Buenos Aires to Mendoza, conversely, provides no view of the Andes.

SURVIVAL TIP

Do not attempt to bring through customs at Santiago airport any foodstuffs, such as cereals, fruit and dairy products. The airport has sniffer dogs and x-ray carousels that will find these. There are hefty fines for bringing in such items.

From Santiago by land

Some parties land in Santiago, then travel by bus over the Andes to Mendoza, stopping off to look at the mountain en route, and returning to the Andes after a day or so in Mendoza. The road journey is a round trip of 540km, which can be rather tedious, especially if all it achieves is a brief look at the mountain. A stop to trek up to the statue of Christ the Redeemer, or to watch river rafting would provide welcome breaks.

Exiting Aconcagua to Santiago may appear to be a simple matter, since the mountain is as close to the Chilean capital as it is to Mendoza, but this is not the case. Buses from Mendoza are either non-stop to Santiago or they stop only at Uspallata, an hour back down the road. These buses are infrequent (three per day) and usually full. They need to be booked in advance. Expect to spend up to 6 hours at the border going through customs and passport control.

SURVIVAL TIP

Travelling from Aconcagua direct to Santiago can be a frustrating and long trip. It is better to go back to Mendoza and fly.

SURVIVAL TIPS

Argentina is weighed down in bureaucracy and every human activity has a law/regulation attached to it involving endless forms. Do not go for your permit without the necessary clearance papers from your trekking company, proof of payment for the permit and your passport.

You do not pay the issuer of the permit. You pay in a Pago Facil. You can pay up to 24 hours before applying for the permit. There is a Pago Facil in Carrefours that is seldom busy.

Once the permit is issued you have 48 hours to enter the park.

Visas, passports and permits

Visas are not required from any Western or first world country to enter either Chile or Argentina. For Chile visas are required from Russia, a number of Central American countries, Korea and former communist countries. In both countries the traveller's passport must have at least six months remaining, and generally entry to the country is restricted to 90 days.

There are restrictive rules for guides on the mountain. If you are being paid to lead people then there are requirements you have to meet.

Before entering Aconcagua Provincial Park trekkers must have a permit and permits are issued in Mendoza, at the Subsecretario de Turismo. You must present yourself in person, fill in forms and show your passport.

The Subsecretario de Turismo is located in the Tourist Office building on Av San Martin, near Garibaldi (on the same side of the street, and close to MacDonald's). You need to pay the permit fee before they issue the permit. The fee is paid to a Pago Facil, an agency that takes the cash (government officials are not allowed to handle cash). You need to bring proof that you have employed the services of a trekking company, or, if you have decided to travel without such services, you will have to pay a higher charge. Of course you will need your passport.

The cost of permits depends on the activity, length of stay in the park, the route you have chosen, and whether it is high, low or medium season. The table sets out the charges that were set in 2016/17.

The rates quoted in the table are in US dollars and apply to foreigners, for the 2016/2017 season. As you can see, it is more expensive to climb via the Vacas Valley (goodness knows why). There is no difference

Checking the permits at Punta de Vacas

in the cost of permits in the medium season and the low season. Although the costs are quoted in dollars you can only pay with pesos, and the government decides what the exchange rate is. Argentineans pay approximately

COST OF PERMITS FOR ACONCAGUA NATIONAL PARK

Season	Dates	Horcones	Vacas Valley	Long trek	Short trek
	Maximum days in park	*20 days*	*20 days*	*7 days*	*3 days*
High	15 Dec–31 Jan	$800	$945	$233	$116
Medium	1 Dec–14 Dec and 1 Feb–20 Feb	$582	$727	$204	$102
Low	15 Nov–30 Nov and 21 Feb–15 Mar	$582	$727	$204	$102
Winter	All except above	$944	Excluded	$305	$131

one-third of this. Other Latin Americans pay half.

Permits are issued Mondays to Fridays from 8am to 6pm, and on Saturdays and Sundays from 9am to 1pm. The centre is closed on Christmas Day and New Year's Day.

Your permit becomes a record of your movements and health in the park. At the park entrance and at each campsite you must check-in and check-out. Your saturated oxygen and heart rate are recorded on the permit. Each trekker is issued with a refuse sack, which must be brought back out, full. At the basecamps a second sack is issued, this to be used for removing excrement. Out-of-season permits are the same cost as high season permits. Daily permits can be purchased at the Horcones ranger station.

If you stay longer in the park than the designated number of days you will be charged a further full permit cost. If you purchase a trekking permit and climb higher than basecamp you will be faced with a fine of two times the ascent permit cost.

Insurance

Undertaking an expedition such as this brings many risks, and insurance against them is to be highly recommended.

If the camp doctor orders your evacuation then the helicopter ride out is free of charge. If you elect yourself to be evacuated, or if you do not consult the doctor with regard to your condition, you will have to pay $2,500. There has been some confusion about this, due to lack of clarity on behalf of the administration, resulting in reports that even if the doctor ordered it you had to pay the helicopter fee regardless.

Leave No Trace policy

The park authorities have become very strict on controlling interference with the environment, on keeping the park clean and controlling waste. A major review and policy statement was produced in 2007, which formulated on-the-spot fines for various offences.

Up to 500 pesos may be imposed for:

- not using designated toilets
- burning native wood, or starting fires outside of designated areas
- burning garbage or polluting rivers
- bringing into the park domestic animals, plants or exotic animals

Up to 1000 pesos may be imposed for:

- throwing garbage about
- loss of the prescribed refuse sack
- damaging wildlife or plants

Rangers are under orders to be proactive in the camps. They will severely reprimand those urinating in any place other than the designated toilets; they will point out garbage or material that may be susceptible to being blown away.

Motivation

To climb a mountain such as Aconcagua is a major life commitment, one to be taken most seriously. Once that decision is made you must realise that there will be multiple decisions that you must make, many things to do and numerous checklists to go through, to ensure the success of the mission. Failure to attend to one of these may be the difference between success and failure.

You are going to have to prepare your body physically and your mind psychologically. You will need to ensure that you have all the necessary and correct equipment. When you are on the mountain you will need to take care to eat the right foods, drink adequate water and look after your other bodily needs.

If you set out assuming that someone else is going to take care of any of these essentials you have started off badly.

Teamwork

You will not achieve this particular goal on your own, so you must commit to being part of a team or a partnership. That has to be a full commitment on both sides. You are likely on summit day to be paired, so choose your partner carefully. They must have similar abilities to you. Build a good relationship with your guide if you have hired one. If you are not part of a group team up with a good climber and build a rapport with them.

When it comes to the crunch on summit day, you must be prepared to turn around to assist your team/partner, and you must be confident that they are of the same persuasion.

Essential gear

Down in Mendoza or Santiago, before and after the climb, shorts, T-shirts and light summer clothing will be the attire. This is the middle of summer. Even at night the temperature will be in the low twenties. The summer months in Mendoza may produce a downpour, but this is so rare as to be ignored.

For the walk in to basecamp shorts and T-shirts will again be appropriate, but warmer clothing and waterproofs should be in your rucksack. Sun protection during the 2–3 day walk should not be underestimated. The searing sun on your back will be relentless. A cool full-sleeve dry flow top and a similar pants may be more appropriate than a vest and shorts as sun protection. Dust storms are common in the Horcones Valley, and windblown sand is a feature everywhere, so bring a mouth and nose shield.

Your summer clothing can be stored at basecamp. It will be warm in the middle of the day, but the temperatures in the morning and afternoon will require warmer clothing.

There are a number of items of non-standard gear that are required on Aconcagua:

- doubled plastic boots
- down jacket
- crampons
- ice axe
- Harness
- -18ºC sleeping bag
- sleeping mattress
- pee bottle
- a length of 9mm rope 15m long
- disposable hand warmers (eight)
- disposable toe warmers
- plastic cup, sharp knife, spoon, thermos flask

Your shell jacket should have a wind shield that will cover your nose. On summit day you will likely start your ascent with the shell jacket on over your down jacket, with your bandit scarf covering your mouth and

Essential gear: double (or triple) plastic boots, down jacket, ice axe, crampons

nose and the shell jacket providing extra wind protection. Balaclava hats are less popular because they restrict air flow.

A down jacket is an essential item of clothing for the long cold evenings at basecamp and above. The down jacket will likely be slept in as a supplement to the -18ºC sleeping bag at the top camp. There is a wide range of down jackets on the market which differ in fill type (synthetic or natural) natural, fill power, ratio of down to feathers and jacket construction. Generally the more expensive the jacket the better it will be. One with a fill power of 700 or more, with a down:feather ratio of 90:10 and made by a well-known company could be several times the cost of a cheaper synthetic version. On Aconcagua it is most unlikely that the jacket will get wet (and therefore lose its insulation), so the natural down will be quite suitable. There is a fine balance, however, between taking a top-of-the-range down jacket and being too hot inside it.

Similarly double plastic boots are essential above basecamp. Leather boots will freeze. There are varieties of insulated leather boots that will be adequate at basecamp and the lower camps. This is provided that the boots are taken into the tent at night and that they are left in the sun in the morning to thaw. However, for the top camps there is no substitute for the double plastics. Virtually every climber on Aconcagua wears them. Indeed some walk in from the

Be prepared for heavy snow

roadhead in the double plastics, dispensing with the weight of trekking boots. The rangers now list double plastic boots and crampons as compulsory above the basecamps.

There is now a wide variety of double (and indeed triple) plastics: the degree of insulation varies; there are types with combined gaiters; some have laces, others zips. A zip is much easier to open and close with heavy gloves. As with down jackets invariably the more you spend the better quality you will get.

As you ascend to the higher camps it is much colder and windier. Most climbers only bring the double plastics. The inner boot will be kept on your feet during the night at top camp. Wind bloc fleeces are essential, but as soon as the sun sets, you will need your down jacket.

For summit day you must be prepared to set off in the dark when the temperature will be at least -10°C, and the chill factor from the wind will decrease the temperature significantly. As the day progresses the temperature will rise, so that a layering system for all parts of the body should be automatic. A balaclava and wool hat, or a bandit scarf, and several layers of gloves are required. The morning temperature may be so severe that you will need to wear your down jacket until dawn. Small lithium disposable hand warmers, slipped into the palm of your gloves can be a most beneficial source of heat on a cold morning. Similarly toe warmers are so thin that they take up no room in your boots.

Your ice axe, harness and crampons may only be required for summit day. Some guides will dispense with a harness, because they can put together an adequate makeshift harness from a length of rope. The pee bottle (with a funnel for ladies) is required to obviate the need to exit the tent at the higher altitude.

The ground surface on the mountain is stony. In all the campsites tents will be pitched on this stony ground, too hard to pierce with timber or steel pegs. Tents will be held down with boulders that are plentiful. Mattresses to alleviate the uneven, rough surface are a necessity.

Items of standard gear that you will need include a pair of walking sticks, two pairs of category 4 sunglasses, walking boots, a 40l daypack, an 80l rucksack, sun hats, bandanas or wind/dust shields, and gaiters to keep the snow out of your boots.

SURVIVAL TIP

A satchel that slips into the top of the rucksack, and that can take your precious items, such as your passport, airline ticket, camera, is most convenient. Around the city and the campsites, it is better than an awkward rucksack.

It is likely that only your large rucksack will be taken above basecamp. This is because daypacks are inadequate in volume for carrying loads from camp to camp, and bringing the daypack for summit day may be seen as a luxury. The large rucksack is the one therefore that will be used on summit day. So, if your style is to have many attachments to the final assault rucksack, it should be made ready at basecamp. In particular your rucksack must have attachments for an ice axe, crampons and walking sticks.

Mules and porters

A mule will carry your gear into basecamp. The mule will stop at the intermediate camps in the valley approach, so that your mattress and sleeping bag and anything heavy can be with the mule. A sturdy gear bag is recommended as it will suffer considerable abuse on the back of the mule.

Mules do not go above basecamp. You may hire a porter to carry your gear, or your guide may suggest to the team the use of one or more porters.

COSTS FOR PORTERS IN 2017 (US$)				
Level	Horcones side		Vacas Valley side	
Weight	20kg	10kg	20kg	10kg
Basecamp to Camp 1	$155	$105	$220	$135
Camp 1 to Camp 2	$245	$150	$330	$205
Camp 2 to Camp 3	$300	$185	$410	$255
Complete round trip	$1,000	$625	$1,260	$780

Before 2009 there were no porters. Climbers were required to carry their own gear, as well as food, tents and camp equipment. That was also advantageous in the acclimatisation process. Now, the hire of porters has become quite popular, although it is expensive. The table shows the 2017 costs.

SURVIVAL TIP

Decide at basecamp whether to hire porters or not. If you carry your gear as far as Camp 2 and need a porter to assist you up to Camp 3, then you pay the same cost as if you had hired him at basecamp.

On the valley approaches rivers have to be crossed. There are two bridges in the Horcones valley and one in the Vacas Valley where the river is deep, but it is still necessary to cross a number of times over the shallower sections. Gore-Tex boots and a pair of walking sticks will be invaluable. In the Vacas Valley between Casa Piedra and Plaza Argentina you will have to make two deep river crossings. A pair of plimsolls or runners may be useful for these crossings, because the water is ice cold and the riverbed is quite uneven. If you opt to pay the exorbitant cost of being carried over the Vacas River on a mule you will still get wet 2km further up when you have to cross the Relinchos River.

You will want to refine your gear so that it is as light as possible. Here are a few tips:

- At basecamp there will be ample time to wash your clothes, and

Crossing the Relinchos River

the drying conditions will be ideal. Even heavy woollen socks will dry under the sun and wind in a few hours.

- High on the mountain sweat is not an issue. Few will have the energy or inclination to brave the cold to change regularly.
- If crampons and ice axes are items that must be acquired then check out the various weights. Some manufacturers, such as Camp and Cassin, produce lightweight gear.
- Western airlines tend to have a lenient approach to excess baggage. This is not the custom in South America. At over $33 per excess kilogram, you could face a hefty bill on your home journey.

SURVIVAL TIP

If you write a diary, ballpoint pens are very susceptible to freezing at high altitude. Keep them warm. Fountain pens are less susceptible, but bring a pencil, just in case.

The medical kit

There are a few items that may not be standard that should be included in the medical bag:

- Sun protection factor 50 or better will be required high up the mountain, and factor 20 for the valley approach.
- The wind will dry and chaff your lips. You will need cream

protection and repair. Lip healing ointment is a most sought after product at the roadhead as climbers recover from their summit attempt.

- Bowel-release and bowel-stop pills should be included.
- Facial wipes will help prevent you from getting too dirty and smelly where water is scarce or stripping off is not an option.

The altitude has differing effects on people, and strangely seems to affect the young more than the mature. Headaches, feelings of nausea and sickness are common and few will escape without some discomfort.

There is a diversity of opinion on the use of Diamox (medical name acetazolamide). It was originally prescribed for glaucoma and has been found effective in alleviating altitude sickness. The medication generally comes in 250mg tablets. A typical daily dose is half a tablet twice daily.

Medical opinion is that the medication can do no harm. It has even been suggested that doubling or tripling the dose is better, but Diamox has side effects. It causes tingling of the tips of the fingers and toes (which should not be misinterpreted as frostbite in the hallucinatory periods on summit day)! A secondary side effect is tenderness in the fingers and toes that can linger for a few weeks after medication has ceased. It also increases dehydration and, on an arid mountain like Aconcagua, this is a significant issue.

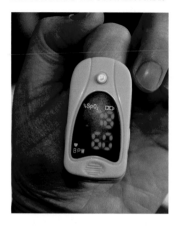

An oximeter measures saturated oxygen and heart rate

It is important to drink copious amounts of liquid when you are at high altitude. Four to five litres per day should be regarded as a minimum. Very often simply the immediate drinking of a litre of water can dispel a headache or a nausea attack. Guides will recommend that people taking Diamox should aim for six litres a day.

Liquids can be spread between water, tea or coffee, juices, soups and so on. Of course, the more you drink, the more you need to urinate. This is not a problem during the day, but at night dressing up to go out in the cold air is not to be recommended – hence the need for a dedicated pee bottle. Experience has shown that the pee bottle should be at least one-and-a-half litres, or alternatively, two

one-litre bottles, and that it should have a wide brim. Collapsible pee-bottles are most useful. Pee-bottles of the same shape/size as drink bottles are obviously not a good idea.

Other preparations

Aconcagua is a difficult mountain and hence requires considerable preparation.

- A superior level of fitness is essential to success. Summit day requires stamina and endurance – in fact pure, brute doggedness. Spurts of training will obviously be inferior to long bouts in the hills, on the road or in the gym.
- You must also be used to, and able to deal with, severe cold. The best way to be prepared for the cold is to have a fit body that has trained regularly in cold and wind-chilled conditions.
- Feet do not break in double plastic boots, the boots break in the feet. Your feet should be accustomed to the rigidity of the boots, especially at the heels and ankles.
- Fitting, removing and refitting crampons should be second nature. On summit day you may need to put them on in the dark, so you should learn to strap them tight.
- There may be a minor degree of rope work, so that familiarity with knots and hooking up are important.

Getting ready for summit day should start before the expedition begins, and should be reassessed at basecamp. Have a checklist of clothing and gear, from head to feet. A simple deficiency that may not matter elsewhere could be the difference between summiting and failure. What will you eat? Don't rely on someone handing you a suitable package for the day, or being able to put a suitable package together. Consider bringing a container from home with food that is non-perishable, can be eaten if frozen, and does not require excessive chewing. The sort of meal-replacement drinks served in old folks' homes, are an option, for instance. Jelly babies, mint chocolate and the like are nourishing and require little effort to eat. But, remember that foodstuffs such as cheese, fruit and cereals cannot be taken into Chile.

These are perhaps the special requirements of Aconcagua. Spending two to three weeks in a tent, living out of a rucksack, caring for your feet, reading, eating and stumbling around by head torch are discomforts that can be learned.

ACCLIMATISATION

Getting used to thin air

Perhaps the most important element in a successful expedition on such a high mountain is acclimatisation. The longer you spend either at basecamp and the lower camps or at other high elevations, the better you will be at high altitude.

Acclimatising on another mountain, such as Vallecitos or El Plomo, can be particularly interesting.

Adjusting the crampons at basecamp

However, this will involve additional organisation, time and expense that you may not want to be burdened with. Trekking in and around the provincial park is an easy alternative. Professional guiding companies, recognising the great advantage of pre-acclimatisation, are offering packages of two peaks in the Andes, such as Vallecitos-Aconcagua or El Plomo-Aconcagua.

Some trekking companies offer an extended Normal Route approach: at Confluencia a day is spent climbing to Plaza Francia (4000m); at Plaza de Mulas another day is spent climbing Cerro Bonete (5004m).

As soon as you get off the bus at Los Penitentes or Puente del Inca the thin air becomes apparent. Breathlessness follows even minor degrees of physical effort. It takes time to become accustomed to this. A slow build-up is recommended. Early exertions can lead to nausea and sickness. However, there is equally little point in being too careful, in taking things too easy. You must gauge how your own body is adjusting and if exertions are showing no ill effects then you should push yourself further.

At the permit office there is an excellent booklet available free of charge that provides information on the provincial park. Contained in the booklet is a guide to altitude ailments. This awards points for medical/physical conditions and recommends appropriate treatment.

Saturated oxygen

As part of its services in policing the Aconcagua provincial park the local government in Mendoza sponsors

An expedition team gets ready at Punta de Vacas

ASSESSING ALTITUDE EFFECTS

Symptoms
- Headache, nausea, loss of appetite and dizziness are allotted **1 point**.
- Vomiting and headaches that are resistant to aspirin/paracetamol are allotted **2 points**.
- Shortness of breath at rest, abnormal fatigue and a low urine volume are allotted **3 points**.

Recommended treatment
- For up to 3 points aspirin or paracetamol is the recommended treatment, with plenty of water.
- From 3 to 6 points it is recommended that ascending ceases, that the climber rests, drinks and takes paracetamol/aspirin, again with copious amounts of water.

Above 6 points the climber is advised to descend.

BREAKFAST AT LOS PENITENTES

When the early bustle of climbers at the hotel had subsided there were two British climbers remaining. Both had been forced to abandon their climb prematurely.

Alan from Leeds, who was in his forties and had been to an altitude of 3600m before coming to Aconcagua, had come down from Camp Canada suffering from pulmonary oedema. His breakfast companion, Richard from Reading, was a little younger. He had been brought down from Nido de Condores with cerebral oedema. They both described their experiences.

Alan had no difficulty on his initial visit to Camp Canada. It was when the team moved there to sleep that he found breathing difficult. He was sick and had chronic diarrhoea. When he arrived down at Plaza de Mulas the doctor recorded his saturated oxygen at only 63 per cent and ordered him airlifted out immediately. He recounted how the pilot had great difficulty with the helicopter in the wind, trying to avoid hitting the sides of the valley. Alan had had a bad night in Los Penitentes and was waiting for transport down to Mendoza.

Richard, on the other hand, had made a complete recovery, had eaten dinner the night before and was tucking into a hearty breakfast. His transport out from Plaza de Mulas was by mule.

The doctor checks saturated oxygen at basecamp

of haemoglobin molecules that carry oxygen could, theoretically, be as high as 100 per cent, but, practically, a little less than this. As one ascends it is natural for some of the molecules not to carry oxygen. However, the higher the number that do carry oxygen the better.

TARGET SATURATED OXYGEN LEVELS	
Altitude (m)	Target % SPO_2
zero	97
1500	93
2000	92
4000	88
5000	83
6000	77

medical tents at Plaza de Mulas and Plaza Argentina where climbers are invited to be checked before they ascend.

The most important aspect of this check is one's saturated oxygen level. This is normally done with a small pulse oximeter. The device is placed over the index finger. It transmits red and infrared light through the finger and detects fluctuating signals caused by blood flow. The ratio of the fluctuation of the red and infrared light signals is used to calculate the blood oxygen saturation ($\%SPO_2$).

Haemoglobin molecules in the blood carry oxygen. For a healthy person at rest at sea level the percentage

At the basecamps, where the altitude is approximately 4250m, a $\%SPO_2$ in the upper 80s is desirable, and some will register over 90. A count under 80 will generally be accompanied by advice to stay at basecamp, relax and drink. A count of less than 70 may come with a recommendation, or indeed an order, to descend.

Cold acclimatisation

If you are an experienced climber you will have been in cold situations on mountains before. You will be aware how far you may allow your hands and feet to suffer cold, knowing that they will eventually return to normal albeit with a sharp pain. You will need this experience for Aconcagua, so that you can tell when you are within your limits and when you have overstepped the mark. You should be able to recognise when your fingers and toes are numb that they will return to normal eventually and that this will be accompanied by this sharp pain. You will be experienced to know that if that situation does not right itself then you must take measures to remedy the situation (see later under 'Dealing with Problems').

GUIDES AND TREKKING COMPANIES

Guides and their necessity

With only the simple word Aconcagua search engines on the internet will display countless companies and individuals who provide guided tours up the mountain. You have the choice of joining a group in your own country, joining a group in Mendoza organised by local Argentineans, or simply going solo.

There is no requirement to hire a guide, and a significant number of climbers and trekkers opt to travel unaccompanied. Mules can be hired on an individual basis at the roadhead, or in advance through the mule companies. At Confluencia and Plaza de Mulas there are restaurants (fairly limited and basic). However, there are no shops on the mountain, so all provisions for the higher camps must be taken.

There are great advantages in hiring a local guide, or joining a locally organised group. The guides know the mountain, speak the language, and most importantly, can read the weather. When mini crises arise, as they often do, a local guide's help can be invaluable. For the local guide the mountain is his livelihood; guiding is his profession. They will have summitted many times. Altitude will have little effect on them. The various guides know one another, so that when one runs out of an essential commodity he knows that he can get help.

Local guides will know the medical doctor on duty, and will know how to raise him in an emergency. If you climb unguided, you need to be reasonably confident that altitude will not cause a crisis for you. Guides will help unguided travellers in an emergency, but with a degree of reluctance. Your guide will discourage you from inviting unguided travellers to accompany the trek, no matter how friendly they are.

The tour operators on the mountain provide toilet facilities for their clients. This is a much more convenient service than collecting your waste and carrying it in your refuse sack or trying to purchase latrine facilities at the basecamp and above.

A word of warning: if you are proposing to hire a guide then pick your guide carefully. A bad guide may be worse than no guide.

Choosing a guide or an expedition organiser

A licensed guide in Argentina must undergo two periods of training, each 20 weeks long, one during the summer and the other during the winter. These guides will have a comprehensive medical kit, including stethoscope, syringes and bandages.

The Mendoza government website provides a list of approved mountain guides.

The larger operators have permanent compounds at the main campsites. When you arrive with your guide the tents are already in place, inside an area that includes the mess tents. Indeed, it is now common to provide actual beds with mattresses. Other climbers may have to clear stones and perch wherever there is space available.

With guides and with permanent compounds the premier operators can take a party up one route and return a different route. They will also tailor their service to the traveller's requirements. A popular service that is available is to arrange pick-up from the airport, hotel in Mendoza, transportation to and from the mountain, and a mule service, but no mountain guide.

In selecting a guide the following obvious questions should be asked:

- How many days are allowed to the summit? Are there any spare days? This is most important. Some guides have little motivation to take climbers to the summit. They have the attitude that the climber may accept that they were not capable or ready, when in fact, they were given inadequate time by the guide to acclimatise.

- What is the ratio of guides to trekkers? A ratio of one guide for every three trekkers should be regarded as a minimum, especially for summit day. There must be adequate guides to bring down people who cannot go on.

- Are the guides licensed?

- How many times has the guide(s) summitted?

- What medical equipment will the guide have – Diamox, saturated oxygen monitor, bowel control tablets, syringes and so on. Some guides take a cylinder of oxygen for emergencies on summit day.

- Will the guide have a radio that can raise basecamp and the doctor?

- What food will be provided – normally, and on summit day?

- What is the hotel accommodation in Mendoza – single or double and what standard?

- Tents – how many to a tent and how big are the tents?

- What are the extra costs for any special arrangements – for instance, going up one route and returning a different route or visiting the Christ the Redeemer Statue or Plaza Francia and/or Cerro Bonete for acclimatisation?

Some operators advertising on the internet offer a package that takes 15 days. This is much too optimistic for those who have no acclimatisation. The inevitable result may be that the summit attempt fails, or that the operator claims an extra premium if the expedition time is extended.

The Mendoza Government website lists the companies providing services in the park. The two biggest trekking companies are Inka Expediciones and Fernando Grajales. Aymara used to be a significant group, but it has changed name to AMG and is no longer a big player. Aconcagua Express and Lanka are minor players. On average, about 5 per cent of trekkers/climbers only hire the very basic of services which would include a mule to basecamp, and toilet services in to and including basecamp.

The duration of the typical itinerary should be regarded as a minimum

for those who are not acclimatised. An extra day at Puente del Inca to go to the statue of Christ the Redeemer, and another from Confluencia to Plaza Francia, will assist with acclimatisation.

A better plan, better use of time and money, with acclimatisation on another mountain, is set out below. You will have tested yourself before the big event. If you do not succeed in scaling Vallecitos it is no loss, since it was not your main goal.

Without a guide

Well prepared seasoned travellers may want to climb the mountain without a guide, some even without a mule, and there is no restriction on them so doing. In fact travelling alone can have many benefits – it reduces costs significantly, you eat what and when you want, and

TYPICAL ITINERARY FOR THE VACAS VALLEY ROUTE

Day 1	Arrive Mendoza	**Day 11**	Rest Day
Day 2	Obtain permit and travel to Puente del Inca	**Day 12**	Move to Camp 2
		Day 13	Rest Day
Day 3	Start trek: Punta de Vacas to Pampa de Leñas	**Day 14**	Move to Camp Cólera
		Day 15	Summit Day
Day 4	Pampa de Leñas to Casa Piedra	**Day 16**	Spare Day
		Day 17	Descend to Basecamp
Day 5	Casa Piedra to Plaza Argentina	**Day 18**	Basecamp to Intermediate Camp
Day 6	Rest Day	**Day 19**	Intermediate Camp to Roadhead
Day 7	Visit Camp 1		
Day 8	Rest Day	**Day 20**	Transport to Mendoza
Day 9	Move to Camp 1	**Day 21**	Flight home
Day 10	Visit Camp 2 Guanacos		

TYPICAL ITINERARY USING THE NORMAL ROUTE

Day 1	Arrive Mendoza	**Day 11**	Walk in to Confluencia 3420m
Day 2	Obtain permits. Travel to Vallecitos 2900m	**Day 12**	Walk to Plaza de Mulas 4365m
Day 3	Short acclimatisation treks in Vallecitos. Rope and crampon trials	**Day 13**	Rest day
		Day 14	Move to Camp Canada 5055m
Day 4	Short acclimatisation treks in Vallecitos 2980m	**Day 15**	Move to Nido de Condores 5580m
Day 5	Trek to Piedra Grande in Vallecitos 3500m	**Day 16**	Rest day
Day 6	Trek to El Salto 4200m	**Day 17**	Move to Cólera 5850m
Day 7	Trek to La Hoyada 4500m	**Day 18**	Summit day and return to Cólera
Day 8	Summit day to Vallecitos 5770m	**Day 19**	Spare day
Day 9	Return to Vallecitos centre	**Day 20**	Return to Plaza de Mulas
Day 10	Travel to Los Penitentes and make ready for Aconcagua	**Day 21**	Return to Penitentes
		Day 22	Return to Mendoza
		Day 23	Flight home

you are not hampered by the inability or pace of fellow travellers.

At the permit office a question on the application form will ask about a guide. This can be ignored. There will be no cross examination on your skill or abilities. At the campsites that have rangers on duty it is necessary to present your permit, and also your passport.

On the road and in the mountain parks there are no great dangers, no history of highwaymen, and the locals are usually very friendly. Language will be a barrier, but not an insurmountable one.

It will be most important that a detailed checklist is made of essential items for the trek. On the mountain cooked food can be purchased at the basecamps, but otherwise there will be no means of acquiring foodstuffs or fuel except through barter with others.

The arrieros

The men who handle the mules on Aconcagua are known as *arrieros*. Some work for the big mule operators, but most are freelance agents hired on a weekly basis. Tremendously loyal to each other and their trade, they are all from

The arrieros – muleteers by day, cooks in the evening, gauchos in the winter.

the plains of Argentina, where they spend the winters herding cattle.

Some will consider them cruel to the mules they handle. However, in the author's experience, they are a hard-working group of men with a wonderful sense of humour. Mules are stubborn animals that have to be continually controlled. A mule cannot be coaxed into action. Mules in the mountains are relatively valuable – the same value as a horse. Whereas a horse generally has to be fed in these arid lands, a mule will generally fend for itself, eating almost anything. There is a shortage of donkeys in Argentina, so that mules are becoming scarce.

The arrieros carry their mate in a satchel that is strewn across the horse. The yerba mate will be on one side, possibly with a separate pouch for sugar, and the gourd and bombilla on the other side.

MATE

Mate is South American tea. Made simply from a chopped up grassy herb and hot water it is drunk from a small vessel, or gourd, through a metal filter, or bombilla. The grass, or yerba mate, is grown in northern Argentina, southern Paraguay and Bolivia. Packed in 1kg bags, it contains natural minerals and vitamins.

The custom of mate is popular in southern Brazil, Peru and Uruguay and is a national obsession in Argentina. Only a little is consumed in Chile.

When mate is taken one person will be in control. They will prepare the initial mixture, taste it and pass it around. The gourd will always be passed back to the controller. To pass it directly to someone else is impolite. The taste is very bitter, but many add sugar to reduce this bitterness. A gourd filling will last from 10 to 30 water toppings. The advent of hot water flasks has provided a great new convenience to the taking of mate.

Mate is now available in tea-bag format, and is being sold all over the world. It is to be hoped that it will not entirely replace the traditional custom of drinking mate in a group with a common gourd.

The arrieros' diet is meat, and plenty of it, cooked on an open fire, eaten, fat and all, with a large sharp knife that they carry in a pouch at their back.

The first arriero to serve on Aconcagua was called Pasten. He assisted both Gussfeldt and later Fitzgerald in their expeditions. One of his descendants works today as an arriero on the mountain.

Hiring mules

Mules can be hired at the roadhead or at the basecamps. It is generally the custom to contract for a round trip from the roadhead to basecamp and back. Prices will vary considerably.

A mule should take no more than 60kg, 30kg on each side, and the mule companies may require special rates for loads that do not fit this arrangement. The arrieros jealously reserve the right to decide how loads are distributed, and how they are secured.

An initial rate will be sought for the first mule, and half of this for the next two mules. One arriero can drive no more than three mules, so the cost of the fourth mule may revert to the higher price, the fifth and sixth the lower price, and so on. These rules are not always adhered to, however. You won't know what other arrangements the mule company is making, so where you have paid for, say, two mules, your shipment may be part of an enormous mule train.

Pablo Reguera, guide with 42 successful ascents

Heber Orona, first Argentinean to complete the seven summits

Andy Jones, guide with 43 successful summits

PART 1
THE ASCENT OF ACONCAGUA

The sign at Horcones, with Aconcagua in the background

MENDOZA TO PUENTE DEL INCA

Mendocinos celebrate Christmas at Plaza Independencia

MENDOZA

Mendoza is a bustling city of over 1 million inhabitants. It is a relatively modern city. Founded in the mid 16th century as a province of Santiago in Chile (and named after the then Captain General of Chile), Mendoza was virtually destroyed by the worst earthquake in South American history in 1861. The city was quickly rebuilt, with wide, tree-lined streets, a central plaza and four satellite plazas (named after the countries that helped in the rebuilding).

The French planner of the modern city laid it out in a grid pattern. Each street has a grass margin with trees separating the footpath from the road. In the grass margin there is a deep trench that conveys water, coming down from the Andes, to irrigate the trees.

Mendoza is the centre of wine-making in Argentina. The Mendocinos have been making wine since the foundation of the city in the sixteenth century. Over 70 per cent of Argentina's wines are produced in Mendoza province. Of the many visitors to the city every year the majority come on wine trips, visiting bodegas in and around Mendoza.

From the city centre the snow-capped Andes are clearly visible (though not Aconcagua, which is blocked from view by a range of intermediate mountains). The Andes is

Central Mendoza

the second most important attraction of Mendoza for visitors. However, only a small proportion are here for Aconcagua. Mendoza is at an elevation of 700m.

Maps of the city are available at every hotel reception. Essentially it is laid out on an (almost) north-south axis. The main artery, from the airport south through the city and out towards Chile/Aconcagua/Tupungato is Av San Martin, commonly called the Alameda. From the Alameda going west there is first of all the main city centre, then Parque San Martin which rises up to the Andes.

The city is compact, and most places are reachable on foot. It is user-friendly and it is nearly impossible to get lost. There is a strong police presence, many patrolling on bicycles.

SURVIVAL TIP

From 2pm to 5pm is siesta time in Mendoza, when many businesses and offices are closed.

The water from the Andes is fundamental to the economy and survival of Mendoza. The main river, Rio Mendoza, is dammed at Potrerillos, where much of the solids settle out. From here it is controlled to irrigate the vineyards, the agricultural lands and the city trees and parks. Drinking water is taken from the Rio Blanco below Vallecitos and piped separately to the city.

White water rafting (and kayaking) is an activity that is growing year by year, and the fast-flowing Mendoza river above Potrerillos is ideal.

For the mountaineer the city has all the necessary facilities. Some of the best gear shops in the world are here, although the costs are not low. You can also hire good gear. Supermarkets within the city and on the outskirts have food suitable for camping and internet cafes abound. *Correos* (post offices) and *locutorios* (businesses offering the use of telephones) are alternative, good value options.

Changing money and paying for things

There is little point in discussing exchange rates, and the cost of commodities if you do not handle your money to the best advantage. Cash is king in Argentina. If you pay with a credit card you may be charged an additional 10 per cent (because the recipient is not declaring his full income). If you take money from an ATM expect to pay a hefty charge, possibly as much as 15 per cent. In general, you can only pay for things in shops, taxis, bus stations and the like in pesos. The most popular foreign currency is the dollar, but euros are now equally acceptable. Sterling is the least popular of the major currencies.

The worst place to change money is at the airport. The rate you will get at your hotel will be marginally better. The best rates are from *casas de cambio* (bureau de change), but these are closed on Sundays. You will be approached to enquire if you want to change money. Be aware of rates and negotiate to your advantage. The casas de cambio are all located in and around the tourist/permit office on San Martin. You will need your passport to change foreign currency.

Water and food on the mountain

If you are part of an organised expedition you need not worry about a number of matters, such as water, food and toilet facilities. The trekking company will provide all of your needs. Every morning you will be issued with drinking water; if you are on the move you will get a lunch pack; if you are static a lunch will be cooked for you. You will not have to concern yourself with cooking facilities, foodstuffs, gas, etc. Your trekking company will also give you snack bars, fruit drinks, nuts and the like. However, there may be particular items of food that you like and perhaps you should spend an hour in the Mendoza supermarkets checking them out (see also the recommendations below for food on summit day).

If you are independent it is most likely that you are well used to finding water, gauging how many canisters of gas you will need, how much salt, sugar, tins of food, fruit, etc. to carry. For your six litres of water per day you will need to be particularly careful, watching for sources in streams, noting areas of clean snow.

Buying provisions

The supermarkets of Mendoza are excellent sources of food for the mountain. However, not all stock the specialist items that climbers seek. There are two Carrefours, for instance, one in the centre of the city on Belgrano, the second on Las Heras.

The following suggestions may be helpful:

- The water that is available on the mountain comes from melted snow and ice. It contains no minerals or nutrients. Supplements can be purchased to provide these ingredients. These are in the form of flavoured sachets and are widely available. Trekking companies will issue a selection of these sachets to their clients.
- Powdered food, such as egg, semolina, milk and potato, is a good and palatable form of food that is easily prepared. Powdered egg is not easy to source. Tea bags, coffee, sugar, soup and the like are freely available. Tea or flavoured herbal mixes may be less harsh on the stomach than coffee, particularly taken in large quantities. Bags of muesli and breakfast cereals, including porridge, are popular. Many shops sell an array of nuts that can be added to the muesli.
- Argentinean fruit and vegetables are wonderful. Oranges and grapefruits are relatively large, but not easily damaged, and provide a welcome juice source. The

local tomatoes are particularly large and succulent. A dish of tomatoes and onions, sprinkled with olive oil and a herb-garlic pepper, takes little time to prepare. Fruit and vegetables, however, must be protected from frost. Canned forms are not as nourishing or appetising, and are heavier, but last longer.

- Argentina and Chile produce quality beef and lamb. Getting meat up to basecamp requires an insulated cooler. There is no traffic in live fowl or animals. Tinned meat is the alternative, generally not available in supermarkets, but in the smaller shops. Specialised boil-in-the-bag meals are not easy to find, and ready-meals are of little use without a microwave. Salami and cheese are great for lunch, and can last the whole expedition if they are protected.

- The most popular form of cooking is liquid paraffin via a pressurised bottle. This commodity is cheap and transferable. It is likely to be one of the heaviest loads to be carried. Standard gas canisters are also readily available.

THE ROAD TO PUENTE DEL INCA

There are three roads out of Mendoza going south towards Chile, Aconcagua and Tupungato. The fastest is the *autopista* (motorway). The most interesting, but also the slowest, is the old route through the vineyards, via the suburb of Lujan. Of further interest along this route is the house of Fernando Fader, the great Mendocino artist whose impressionist style made him world famous.

The long distance public buses that travel between Santiago and

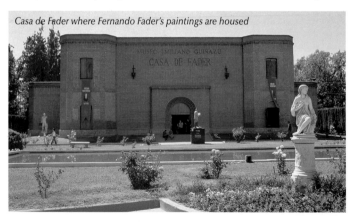

Casa de Fader where Fernando Fader's paintings are housed

The ski resort of Los Penitentes with Tolosa Mountain in the background

Mendoza are of excellent quality and are relatively inexpensive. The buses from Mendoza stop at the town of Uspallata, a dusty town clogged with trucks and buses, at an elevation of 1850m. The town was formerly a centre for iron ore smelting, where cannonballs were manufactured for the army that swept down into Chile to defeat the Spanish. In recent times the area became famous as the location for the making of the film *Seven Years in Tibet*.

There is a road out of Uspallata to the east, not the old road to Mendoza, but another dirt track road south of it. This road leads to The Rock of the Seven Colours, an unusual volcanic landscape, with colours ranging from white to yellow to purple.

On the approach in to Uspallata there is a busy restaurant on the right-hand side that is the best place to eat between Mendoza and Aconcagua. The establishment is called Estancia Elias and is 2km from the village centre. Their *parillada* is particularly good.

There is a regular local bus service (inexpensive, three per day) from Mendoza that stops at Punta de Vacas, Los Penitentes and Puente del Inca. These must not be confused with the long distance buses to/from Mendoza to Santiago, most of which do not stop at all between the two cities, the minority only stopping at Uspallata. The bus station in Mendoza is southeast of the central block (see Mendoza map) on the street extension of Calle Colon. The local buses stop at Punta de Vacas, at Los Penitentes and on the road beside the Horcones ranger station.

The Andinista graveyard

Mendoza to Santiago disused railway

The Mendoza to Santiago Railway is a most interesting feature of the landscape that runs parallel to the road all the way from city to city. It was built between 1890 and 1920 and its scale is an indication of the wealth in the region during that period. There are numerous tunnels and bridges. All of the sleepers on the Argentinean side are timber, but the Chileans opted for steel sleepers in the mountains on their side.

When it opened in the 1920s it carried both goods and passengers along the 350km journey. Subject to regular rockslides and subsidence, the railway required costly maintenance. At Las Cuevas, for instance, the enormous boulders on the line that rolled down in an avalanche are testament to this. Eventually the railway that took so much effort to construct was allowed to fall into disrepair and was closed

permanently in the 1980s. There were allegations at the time that the Chilean dictator, Pinochet, was involved in the largest trucking company, and that this made the decision that much easier.

Nowadays the drone of juggernauts and buses has replaced the noise of steam. In recent times estimates have been prepared to restore the railway, but the $1 billion project (at one stage proposed to be carried out by a Chinese contractor) has stalled. The truckers are a powerful political force.

Los Penitentes

Los Penitentes is the most popular stop for climbers. It is a ski resort with a cable car and a number of hotels. During the summer only one or two establishments are open.

Los Penitentes is at an elevation of 2580m, so that, for those who are not acclimatised, the altitude effects will begin here. It is a good policy to

Old roads and ski paths above Los Penitentes

walk around, even if only to go up and down the road, to start the acclimatisation process.

Puente del Inca

It would be most unfortunate for the traveller to come to Aconcagua and not experience Puente del Inca. The natural wonder of the bridge and its thermal waters should not be missed (in 2017 access to the old hotel and spa was temporarily closed).

Puente del Inca is a better, less expensive, place to stay than Los Penitentes. It is closer to the Horcones roadhead and is a little village full of life. The juggernauts do not even change gear when going through Los Penitentes.

The village takes its name from the bridge over the River Las Cuevas. Only 50 metres from the main road, the bridge is through a wide lane that has souvenir stalls on either side.

Around the bridge the riverbanks are coloured a bright orange by the sulphur from the hot springs. Erected beside the bridge are notices that display how it was formed – an initial ice bridge over the river, an avalanche of boulders that covered the ice, sulphur from the springs cementing the boulders together, then the ice underneath melting.

A hotel was built in 1917, specifically for the clients to take the hot springs, with a tunnel connecting the hotel to the baths under the bridge. The hotel thrived until 1965 when an enormous avalanche destroyed it. The baths themselves, though now disused, can still provide a refreshing hot shower.

Of the places to stay in Puente del Inca the army hostel is worth considering. Over the entrance door to the army barracks (*Ejercito Argentina*) is a sign welcoming all mountaineers. The

The natural bridge over the Las Cuevas River at Puente del Inca

dedicated visitors' hostel, suitable for both sexes, can accommodate 76 visitors in bunk-bedded rooms with separate bathrooms. Though the bedrooms are rather basic, the ground floor reception rooms are spacious and comfortable, and the food is good. This is the cheapest accommodation for Aconcagua.

Between Puente del Inca and Los Penitentes is the Andinistas Graveyard. Many of those buried in the graveyards died on Aconcagua. This is a relatively short walk from Los Penitentes, one that many climbers take. You may walk from Puente del Inca along the old railway (if you do not suffer from vertigo at the bridges) or alternatively along the mule track.

Punta de Vacas, like Puente del Inca, is essentially an army base that caters for long-distance trucks. It has no shop or hotel.

Back towards Punta de Vacas there is a little natural history museum built out of the ruins of an old railway structure. The enthusiastic owner (who speaks no English) has a makeshift array of pulleys and pumps that simulate tectonic plate movement, earthquakes and volcanic action. Well worth the $1 entry.

If you walk back far enough towards Punta de Vacas, at a bend in the road, there is a clear view of Tupungato.

ACONCAGUA ROUTES

The Normal Route

SUMMARY OF CAMPS – NORMAL ROUTE

Camp	Elev	Elev Gain	Distance	Time	Difficulties
Roadhead Horcones	2535	-	-	-	Present permit and passport at Ranger Station
Confluencia	3420	885m	8km	2½ hrs	Easy walk. Hot, no shade
Basecamp Plaza de Mulas	4365	945m	28km	8 hrs	Tough, long day. May have to cross shallow streams. Wind-blown sand. No shade
Canada	5055	690m	3km	5 hrs	Steep, steady climb
Nido de Condores	5580	525m	4km	5 hrs	Steep, steady climb
Cólera	5970	390m	5km	4½ hrs	Tough, though short, climb
Summit	6962	992m	9km	9 hrs	Long trek, initially in the dark, very cold. Canaleta the most difficult part. Descent to Cólera will take 5 hours
Return to Basecamp			12km	6 hrs	Steep in places
Return to Roadhead			36km	9 hrs	Long, energy-sapping walk

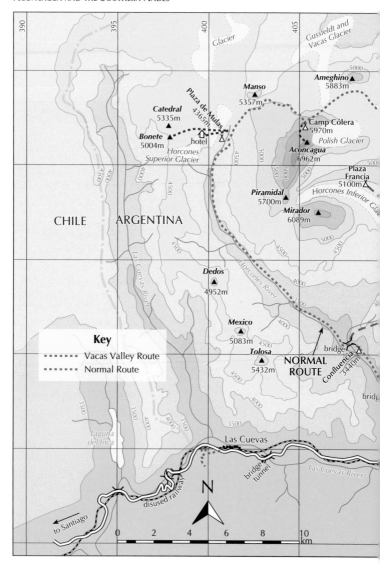

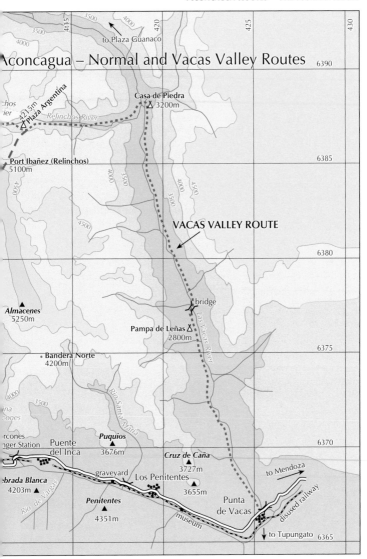

Aconcagua – Normal and Vacas Valley Routes

to Plaza Guanaco

6390

Casa de Piedra
△ 3200m

Relinchos River

△ 4215m Plaza Argentina

Port Ibañez (Relinchos)
5100m

6385

VACAS VALLEY ROUTE

6380

bridge

Pampa de Leñas △
2800m

Las Vacas River

6375

Almacenes
5250m

Bandera Norte
4200m

Rio Santa María

6370

Puquios
▲ 3676m

Puente
del Inca

Cruz de Caña
▲ 3727m

to Mendoza

Ranger Station

Quebrada Blanca
▲ 4203m

Rio de Vargas

graveyard

Los Penitentes

▲ 3655m

disused railway

Penitentes
▲ 4351m

museum

Punta
de Vacas

↓ to Tupungato

6365

The Normal Route

Start	5km W of Puenta del Inca
Distance	36km to basecamp
Time	2 days to basecamp, 12 days minimum in park
Maximum elevation	4365m to basecamp, 6962m to summit
Water sources	None above basecamp

The Ruta Normal begins about 5km west of Puente del Inca, or 10km from Los Penitentes. Off a concrete entrance road there is a gravel car park near a ranger station and a helicopter is permanently parked nearby. This helicopter is used to take medical and emergency supplies to the various basecamps and to airlift sick or injured climbers out. It is in constant use, generally landing at both basecamps at least once every day. Since its introduction in the 1999/2000 season the number of fatalities on the mountain has dropped from seven or eight a year to one or two.

The ranger will check the permits and issue refuse sacks. The non-return of a refuse sack carries a hefty fine. Guides may sometimes take charge of your refuse sack.

The start of the Normal Route at Horcones

There is a dirt track road in for a few kilometres, but its use for vehicles is closed except in emergencies. Two-and-a-half kilometres in is the **lagoon**, where you will undoubtedly want to take more photographs. The road is stony and flat as far as the first footbridge – a gentle introduction to the Ruta Normal. The steel suspension bridge was erected some years ago over the raging torrent below. After the footbridge the path initially follows the river on its eastern bank. Then it leaves the river to rise steeply through a grey limestone boulder field before it eases out to a gentle gradient on the approach to **Confluencia**. ▸

For these first 2 days of the journey to basecamp it will be necessary to carry all that is needed for the night in Confluencia and during the day. The mules will have gone ahead with the main loads.

The Confluencia campsite was moved in 2007, for the second time in eight years. It is now nearly 1km nearer to Horcones and further from Plaza de Mulas. So it is only a short 2 to 2½ hour walk from Horcones. It is now customary for trekkers to have their lunch at Penitentes before starting the walk.

Confluencia campsite

The name 'Confluencia' comes from the confluence of the two rivers, that from the Horcones valley and that from the Lower Horcones Inferior Glacier in the valley above.

*Horcones Inferior
Glacier discharges
north of Confluencia*

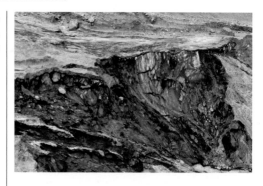

At 3420m (slightly at odds with the camp sign which says 3440m) the Confluencia campsite is an open area, quite windy and very dusty. There is water available, but it generally contains a lot of magnesium, and is not so pleasant to drink. It is advisable to take your own water.

*High above
Confluencia is
Cerro Almacenes
(5250m) with its
horizontally bedded
sedimentary rocks.
In front of it you
may see peregrine
falcons soaring.*

The choice of location for the new campsite, understandably, is a bone of contention between the tour operators and arrieros on one side, and the park rangers on the other side. Some will rest here for a day. Some will trek up to Plaza Francia and return. Those on their way out may only pause to take on water.

From the road head to Confluencia the altitude will have increased from 2580m to 3420m. It will be hot during the day at Confluencia, perhaps as high as 27°C, falling when the sun goes down to perhaps 6°C at night. ◄

SURVIVAL TIP

This will likely be your first experience of the mountain's toilet facilities. The communal, public toilet is supplemented by toilets provided by the various tour companies. The ranger will be vigilant for those too lazy to make the journey to, and then queue outside a busy toilet.

From Confluencia to Plaza de Mulas takes 7–8 hours. Initially the path runs over the river floodplain. Underfoot the ground is a flat walk over gravel. It may be necessary to cross the river depending on the route the river has taken, but generally the path avoids the river. Winds whip up the dust in this open plain, so it's important to have a neckerchief/scarf to protect your mouth and nose.

▶ Throughout the next few hours of walking, Cerro los Dedos (4900m) can be seen up the valley ahead. After passing this peak the path diverges away from the river and the gradient becomes steep.

As you pass the river coming out of valley to the right pause to look at the enormity of the Horcones Inferior Glacier.

Near to basecamp the trail becomes dramatically more challenging. **Plaza de Mulas** is at an elevation of 4365m, and the last few kilometres account for most of the rise in elevation.

At the height of the season expect to find upwards of 100 tents and 50 mess tents, so that the population could be several hundred people. Plaza de Mulas is a relatively sheltered campsite, with good, fresh water.

En route to Plaza de Mulas

Basecamp Plaza de Mulas

A short walk to the west from basecamp is the **Hotel Plaza de Mulas**. This closed in 2009 (the owner no longer paid his taxes and the government seized the building). En route to the hotel you will encounter your first field of penitentes. The walk over to the hotel takes 20 minutes, over undulating ground. For the unacclimatised newcomer it will be an energy-sapping experience.

> **SURVIVAL TIP**
>
> There is mobile telephone coverage at Plaza de Mulas. The larger tour operators also provide internet connections.

There is always at least one independent mess tent at basecamp where you can eat and drink, with burgers, steak sandwiches and beer very popular. Hygiene is not a strong point in these makeshift cafés, however, and there have been incidences of diarrhoea.

Upon arrival at basecamp you need to check in with the ranger and the doctor. The latter will check your heart rate, blood pressure and saturated oxygen. The service is free. Virtually everyone takes at least one day's rest at Plaza de Mulas, some two or more days. The saturated oxygen count may dictate an even longer stay.

The climb of Cerro Bonete (5004m) from Plaza de Mulas is a worthwhile acclimatisation exercise. It will take 4 hours to climb and 2½ hours to descend, so that it is a day's hike. The path is obvious, a guide is not needed, and the gradient is moderate. Walk over to the hotel, then take the path to the north of it. The policeman guarding the hotel will point out the path if there is any doubt.

A cheeky grey-headed sierra finch enters the mess tent looking for food

Above Plaza de Mulas there are three intermediate camps before the summit:

- **Camp Canada** at 5055m,
- **Nido de Condores** at 5580m, and finally
- **Berlin** at 5850m, or **Cólera** at 5970m

Cerro Bonete (5004m) – a 4-hour walk from Plaza de Mulas

The camps at Canada and Nido de Condores are ill-defined, with tents pitched in no particular pattern. At Canada the campsite is south of the route up the mountain, and at Nido the route is through the campsite. At Berlin the camp is on a shoulder of the mountain, and the tents are tightly grouped around a number of wooden huts.

Whereas the trail into Plaza de Mulas is relatively flat, except for the last few kilometres, it changes significantly above the basecamp. Out over the field of penitentes from Plaza de Mulas the route is quite steep and only eases upon reaching **Camp Canada**. ◄

Nido de Condores was elevated in 2002 to somewhat the same status as the basecamps, and now has a resident park ranger. This reflects the numbers who camp there. Some may bypass Camp Canada, and some may make their summit bid direct from Nido, but few bypass Nido.

The ranger here has significant authority. He is required to check on the condition of climbers, and may call to tents. He can order you to descend if he suspects you're in poor medical or physical condition, or if you don't have the proper gear for this altitude.

Halfway between Plaza de Mulas and Canada there is a rocky, isolated area that is known as The Conway Stones, named after 19th-century English scientist and mountaineer, Sir Martin Conway.

Berlin Camp

Heavy snow around Refugio Elena at Camp Cólera

SURVIVAL TIP

None of the upper camps have fresh water, so that snow must be gathered for melting. Berlin can be particularly cramped. Behind most boulders there are the inevitable excrement deposits, so finding fresh, clean snow may require a climb.

Until 2012 Berlin was the most popular camp above 5800m. This is no longer the case, most operators favouring the better sheltered Cólera site. Within the Cólera camp there is an emergency hut that is known as Refugio Elena. This hut was erected by the relatives of Elena Senin, an Italian female climber who died in 2009 (see 'The January 2009 Deaths').

As the altitude increases the night-time temperature and the wind chill become more significant. At base-camp there can be a considerable degree of movement around the camp at night. There will be discussions and the occasional singsong. At the upper camps the cold will

Sunset over Berlin

drive all into their sleeping bags as soon as the sun sets, and few will venture out until the sun once again shines on the tent in the morning.

Up to **Nido de Condores** the emphasis will be on steady trekking, acclimatisation, taking things easy, regular resting, carrying a load up to return and sleep at a lower camp. After Nido that pattern changes. Upon reaching **Berlin** or **Cólera** the focus is on the summit. Spending a rest day at an altitude of in excess of 5800m is not to be recommended. The air is thin, it is difficult to sleep, appetites are poor and the weather can be treacherous. The attitude is to make ready at Berlin or Cólera and set off early the next morning for the summit.

In the late afternoon at Berlin/Cólera climbers will be returning from their summit attempt. Those who have summitted will be in high spirits and may continue their celebrations into the night, much to the annoyance of those who are trying to gain a degree of peaceful repose (sleep might be too much to hope for) before their early morning venture. There will be drama too as anxious eyes watch the skyline at dusk for comrades who are on their way down. There will be the occasional scramble from the camp to help exhausted climbers make it back.

The sunsets at Berlin/Cólera can be spectacular, and well worth staying up for. As every mountain climber knows, the sky at night over such places can be so clear, the stars so vivid.

SUMMARY OF CAMPS – VACAS VALLEY ROUTE

Camp	Elev	Elev Gain	Distance	Time	Difficulties
Roadhead Punta de Vacas	2415	-	-	-	Present permit and passport at Ranger Station
Pampa de Leñas	2800	385m	18km	5 hrs	Medium grade, though undulating, pleasant beside river
Casa de Piedra	3200	400m	17km	5 hrs	Similar to previous day
Basecamp Plaza Argentina	4215	1015m	12km	7 hrs	Cross ice-cold river, then precipitous walk, cross a second river. Steep initially. Steady/medium thereafter
Camp 1	5000	785m	3km	5 hrs	Tough climb through penitentes
Guanacos	5475	475m	4km	6 hrs	Initially tough climb possibly in crampons through snow/ice. Then easy walk
Cólera	5970	495m	4km	4 hrs	Tough, though short, climb
Summit	6962	992m	9km	9 hours	Long trek, initially in the dark, very cold. Canaleta the most difficult part. Descent to Cólera will take 5 hours
Return to Basecamp			20km	7 hours	Long and steep descent, especially coming into basecamp
Return to Roadhead			47km	2 days 9 hours + 4½ hrs	First day is very long to Pampa de Leñas. Two rivers to cross. Second day is short and easy

The Vacas Valley Route

Start	Punta de Vacas
Distance	47km to basecamp
Time	3 days to basecamp, 14 days minimum in park
Maximum elevation	4200m to basecamp, 6962m to summit
Water sources	Streams up to Camp 2

The Vacas Valley Route starts at Punta de Vacas, 7km east of Los Penitentes. Activity at the roadhead is much quieter than further west at the start of the Normal Route.

Steeper and more rugged than the Normal Route, the trail rises and falls with the river, winding over steep scree. There is good shelter from the sun and wind, however. You will be aware immediately of the solitude, interrupted by scurrying lizards and singing birds.

Towards Pampas de Leñas

The initial journey ends at **Pampa de Leñas** after 4–5 hours. Expect the day to be arduous and hot. You will know that you are within 15 minutes of the campsite when you have to cross a fast-flowing stream that has clean drinking water.

Campsite Pampa de Leñas

> Pampa de Leñas is at an elevation of 2800m, so that the elevation gained on the first day is very small. Unlike Confluencia the campsites of Pampa de Leñas and Casa de Piedra have to be dismantled every day, so you may arrive with only the ranger station visible. The area is nestled under high cliffs, sheltered and peaceful. Potable water is available from a tap near the ranger station.

AN ENCOUNTER AT PAMPA DE LEÑAS

Two cockneys were resting at Pampa de Leñas, en route from Plaza Argentina to Punta de Vacas. They were originally three, but one had to be airlifted out due to altitude sickness. The two had reached Camp 2 and were preparing for a summit attempt. It was extremely cold in the early morning,

93

the temperature -15°C. One of them had removed his gloves in order to put on and tie his boots. When he put the gloves back on he could not get circulation back into all his fingers. Nevertheless he started the climb. After an hour he stopped and discussed his problem with the guide. Vain attempts were made to warm his hands, but it was not possible to get the blood in his thumbs to circulate. Eventually he returned to camp, and his comrade proceeded to the summit. Warm water failed to relieve the problem. At base-camp the doctor had bandaged the thumbs, but was doubtful that they could be saved. They were now turning black.

The friends further related how they had been in the company of a Korean on the inward journey from Punta de Vacas. At Pampa de Leñas the Korean had decided to flex his muscles by climbing the cliff above the camp. He had fallen and was seriously injured. They were now informed that the Korean died on the way to hospital.

Bridge past Pampa de Leñas

The trail on the second day to Casa de Piedra is very similar, once again with very little elevation achieved. On the journey you will cross a footbridge 1km north of Pampa de Leñas and later see cattle grazing on the river's edge.

At **Casa de Piedra** you are treated to a wonderful view of Aconcagua from the Polish Glacier side. As you approach the campsite clearing Cerro Ameghino initially comes into view, followed later by the awesome bulk of Aconcagua.

Campsite Casa de Piedra

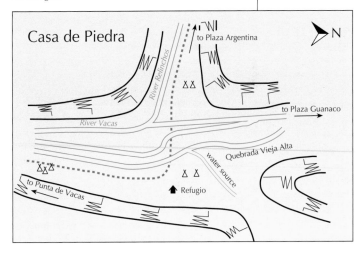

95

Crossing the Rio Vacas at Casa de Piedra

Casa de Piedra, at an elevation of 3200m, is a tight campsite alongside the river. There is a rough stone structure, from which the site gets its name, built into an enormous isolated conglomerate rock on the eastern bank. In and around this stone structure the arrieros will camp. In the past it was permissible to immediately cross the river and camp, so that boots and socks can be dried out by morning, but this is no longer allowed.

The river at Casa de Piedra has many tributaries, so that there are multiple crossings. The water is icy cold, so cold that it hurts. It can be quite deep and you may consider stripping to your underwear. If you decide to arrange for a mule to carry you across in the morning (at a cost of $10) bear in mind that you will nevertheless get wet further up the valley towards Plaza Argentina. So, it is perhaps better to face up to bringing your sandals and carrying your boots, and getting wet like everyone else.

This is the most likely stretch to see guanacos, possibly dead ones, for they are fragile animals prone to falling on these rocky parts.

From Casa de Piedra up the **Relinchos Valley** the trail is tough. ◄ For the first few kilometres there are many

precipitous climbs around the steep sides of the river. Then the trail changes to a gradual gradient. A little over halfway up the valley you can rest and have lunch in a boulder field on the side of the trail.

The route to Plaza Argentina

Plaza Argentina at 4215m is at a slightly lower elevation than Plaza de Mulas. It is a 5–6 hour walk from Casa de Piedra up through the Relinchos River valley. The Relinchos Glacier hangs above the campsite and dictates much of the trail above it. Similar to the Lower Horcones Glacier it is covered in scree. Eventually the glacier gives way to undulating land that leads down into Plaza Argentina.

The camp lies on a glacial moraine so that many of the tents are often hidden from view. Plaza Argentina will have the same facilities, on a smaller scale, as Plaza de Mulas. Here, at the height of the season, there may be up to 50 tents and 15 mess tents. The doctor and the ranger will be here. There is no phone link to the outside world, but there is usually a private cafe.

Basecamp Plaza Argentina

Above Plaza Argentina there are three intermediate camps before the summit. Whereas **Camp 1** has remained popular, the upper camps have changed over time. The traditional route was via **Camp 2** (5830m) and on to either **Berlin** on the Normal Route or **Rocas Blancas** (6095m). The two upper camps at Camp 2 and Rocas Blancas are quite exposed and their use has lost popularity to the more sheltered **Camp Guanacos** (5475m) (sometimes referred to as Camp 3) and **Cólera** (5970m).

The climb from basecamp to Camp 1 is a gruelling 5 hours through fields of penitentes, and over a glacier that has rough scree deposits. Often there is the choice of scrambling over loose gravely moraine or negotiating a way through the penitentes. The eventual approach in to Camp 1 is a left-hand turn over deep snow and ice, entering the camp over a boulder field.

Camp 1 is a linear campsite on a windy shoulder on the mountain, where the tents are protected by walls of stones. Water is available from the icy river that flows alongside. The campsite is long, stretching for half a kilometre and over 50m in elevation.

From Camp 1 to Camp 2 the elevation increases by over 750m, again a tough day's climb taking 5–6 hours. The initial part is over snow that may require crampons. The path zig-zags up to a col at **Portezuelo Ameghino** (5300m). From here to Camp 2 is a further 5 hours of climbing. However, if you choose to go to Camp Guanacos, it is a pleasant 2–3 hour walk.

Negotiating the penitentes above Plaza Argentina

Camp Guanacos

Camp 2 is an open camp with little protection from the wind and sun. Fresh water flows through the icy river beside the camp. Camp 2 is at the edge of the Polish Glacier and is the camp used by those making the Polish Glacier direct ascent.

Above the campsite, under a cliff face, there is a grave to an Argentinean who died in 1983. The grave is rather shallow and portions of his clothes and body are exposed.

From Camp 2 to Rocas Blancas (6095m) it is a mere 3 hours of easy climb, occasionally over ice. The route is around the rear of the mountain. Crampons and an ice axe will be essential to negotiate the short ice field.

Rocas Blancas, also referred to as Piedras Blancas (small rocks as opposed to large rocks), is an exposed site nestled against the white rocks from which it takes its name. There is no water.

Camp Guanacos (5475m) was on a route from Plaza Guanaco (3750m) further along the Rio Vacas from Casa Piedra, but this route is no longer allowed due to protections imposed for the guanacos. From Camp Guanacos to Cólera is a long, gradual climb of 500m.

Cólera campsite

Summit day

The route through the Gran Acarreo

To reach Berlin and/or Rocas Blancas or Cólera from either of the basecamps is only half the work of summiting Aconcagua. The second half is summit day. You must now concentrate all your energies for that last push.

Rocas Blancas is on the Normal Route above Camp Berlin. From Berlin there is an initial steep scramble before you reach the stony path. From Rocas Blancas the trail to the normal route is good and easy.

Independencia is a popular spot for a rest and a drink, perhaps also a convenient place to don crampons, depending on the weather.

Cólera is to the east, slightly higher than Berlin. Where the trails meet the climb is steady to a col where there is a ruined wooden hut known as **Independencia**. ◄ This is at an elevation of 6400m. Some climbers may opt to camp at Independencia and shorten summit day by a further hour or so. This option, and very rare, is only when there is little wind.

The climb from Independencia is steady and traverses up to a ridge known as Cresta del Viento. Here you turn left to cross a very exposed area where the wind is unrelenting. Beyond the Cresta del Viento is the Gran

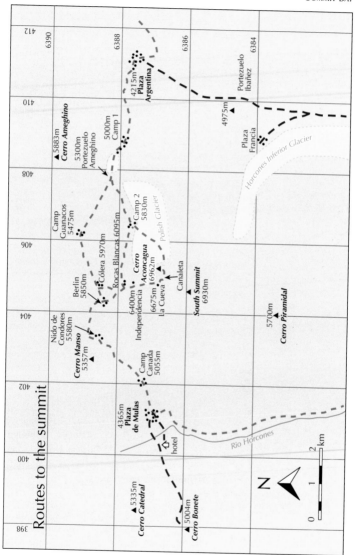

Routes to the summit

Acarreo that leads to the base of the **Canaleta**, at 6675m. The Gran Acarreo is a relatively easy traverse, but the terrain becomes loose underfoot.

To classify the Canaleta as a slagheap is perhaps disingenuous, but most apt. The mixture of loose sand and gravel is frustrating, for with every two steps you take you slide back one. The Canaleta is 400m high and takes several hours to ascend. Near its base there is a shelter under a cliff face, known as **La Cueva**, where climbers leave rucksacks, taking only the bare essentials to the summit. Here guides will encourage climbers to summon up all their remaining strength for this final assault. Occasionally the Canaleta is covered in frozen snow, when it is relatively easy to climb in crampons.

At the top of the Canaleta there is a gentle traverse to negotiate and some large boulders to overcome before arriving at the summit. Above this gentle traverse the ridge is known as the Cresta del Guanaco. It connects the **South Summit** to the north summit. On the north summit, the highest point of the Americas is marked by a simple aluminium cross.

Summit cross

On a clear day views from the summit are stunning. To the south you can see the white mountain of Tupungato. Below is the south face with the Horcones Inferior Glacier and Plaza Francia visible.

Almost every climber brings a memento to the summit – scarves, bandanas, flags and so on – so that, by the end of the season, the tiny aluminium cross can hardly be seen. The ice and snow of the winter, however, is a natural clearer, and, by spring, the cross is restored to its isolation.

View from the summit with climbers on the Canaleta

DEALING WITH PROBLEMS

Wind chill and the cold
For every 100m of altitude gained there will be a drop of between half and one degree in the temperature. Thus, if it is -5°C at basecamp it can be expected to be -25°C approaching the summit. The higher the speed of the wind the greater the wind chill.

WIND CHILL CALCULATOR

Temp/Wind Speed	20km/hr	30km/hr	40km/hr	60km/hr
0°C	-10°C	-12°C	-16°C	-20°C
-10°C	-23°C	-26°C	-33°C	-36°C
-20°C	-33°C	-40°C	-50°C	-55°C
-30°C	-47°C	-55°C	-62°C	-70°C

Exposure of bare flesh to a wind chill of under 20°C for anything but a few seconds will lead to problems, and exposure of the flesh to a wind chill of -30°C at all will lead to frostbite. At high wind chill levels your balaclava or bandit scarf and shield should completely cover your face.

You must keep your fingers and toes moving as much as possible. Stretch them as often as you can. Getting them out of the wind will help enormously. If you feel that you may have been over exposed then try to get some hot liquid inside you, preferably with lots of sugar. Movement will bring a heat flow into the body, but it will use up your store of energy.

Those eight hand warmers that were recommended (see 'Preparations') – four of them were intended for use on summit day, one in each glove early in the morning, refreshed mid morning, while the remaining four were intended for emergencies. If you can get a hand warmer to an affected area it could be the difference between losing a finger or toe.

THE JANUARY 2009 DEATHS

In early 2009 there were four deaths on the mountain in three separate incidences, and within a few days of each other.

The first to die was Stefan, an architect from Cologne in Germany. He had been climbing on the Polish Glacier with a Canadian that he had met at Plaza Argentina. They had set off for the summit together, eventually they split and the Canadian pushed on for the summit while Stefan decided to descend. The weather was poor. Conditions under foot on the glacier were far from ideal, with a soft snow capping in places.

The Canadian eventually succumbed to the weather, and it was as he descended that he noticed an object on the rocks far below him, which turned out to be Stefan's body. This author was on the mountain at the time and came out with the Canadian.

On the same day four Italians – two men and two women – and their guide, Federico Campanini, a young, accomplished mountaineer resident in the US, made it with difficulty to the summit. The weather set in and the five got separated. None returned to camp that night. The next day, during a break in the weather, they were spotted, but again, no one returned to camp. Miraculously, two days after they made their bid for the summit three of them were rescued. One of the women, Elena Senin (38), and the guide, Federico (31), died. The others suffered severe frostbite to their fingers and hands.

On the same day that the Italians were rescued an Englishman, Michael Fleeman (42), died of a heart attack after he had successfully summitted.

It was unusual for four people to die on the mountain in such a few days, and it sent shockwaves through the community. The press in Mendoza gave great prominence to the matter, and senior climbers were interviewed at length. The consensus was that the climbers, other than the last one, should not have been where they were. The two on the Polish Glacier should have known that the underfoot conditions were treacherous, and that the glacier was not suitable to be on that day. The Italians and their guide were too late to reach the summit and should have returned to Berlin when they saw that the weather was closing in.

The death of Campanini is particularly controversial. He had partly descended the Polish Glacier in order to help Elena Senin. The rescuers, some of whom had come from the camps, reached him when he was still alive. A video was taken of him on his hands and knees in the snow, with ropes fixed to him by the rescuers. The six rescuers are seen trying to move him up out of the Polish Glacier to the summit to take him down a safe route. Unfortunately Campanini died of oedema. His father Carlos, who was anonymously given the video, took the rescuers to court citing that they did not do enough for his son (in Argentina there is a law requiring people to help those in danger). The case was dismissed, but the controversy continues. Carlos posted the video on YouTube where it can still be viewed.

The ascent from Camp 1 to Plaza Argentina

In the event of a storm

The golden rule is to stick to whoever you are with. The most likely time for snow to fall is in the afternoon, when people are descending. A complete white out can leave a climber most exposed, so try to team up with others, rope up, and share your decisions.

Getting down safely

Aconcagua is not unlike other high mountains where fatalities are more generally likely to occur on the descent rather than on the ascent. The sense of euphoria may tend to block out the reality that beckons. The mind and body will be tired. Poor weather is more prone on the mountain in the afternoon than in the morning.

Roping up on the Canaleta descent should be mandatory. This is the most dangerous section. On the approach to Berlin there is another dangerous section where a rock outcrop must be negotiated.

The long walk out

Most trekkers will take a day to descend from Berlin/
Cólera to Plaza de Mulas. Similarly, a day is the usual
time to Plaza Argentina. The latter is a longer descent
than the former. Although the climbing is over, and the
air is becoming thicker, the day is a difficult one. All of
the gear that was taken up in loads on previous days must
be taken down now in one load. Those arriving at the top
camps will be pleasantly surprised to be offered excess
food and fuel oil. Guides will bundle food and fuel and
leave it for future visits.

On the track down stumbling and falling will be
inevitable, and here the trekking poles provide good balance. The monotony will be broken by sudden surges as
trekkers throw caution to the wind and virtually ski down
the steeper gravely paths. Your rucksack straps should be
pulled tight into your chest to avoid back strain.

On the Vacas Valley Route the descent is much
slower than the Normal Route. The fields of penitentes

*The arrieros have
an easy ride out*

make coming down slow, and many will reach basecamp late in the day.

The beer at basecamp that was forbidden a week before, that was so expensive a week before, is drunk in copious amounts by descenders. At basecamp every summitter wants to share his euphoria, not only with those in the camp, but with their family at home. Those who failed are already planning their return.

It is a long arduous day from Plaza de Mulas to the roadhead. The trekkers will look in envy at the arrieros on their horses. The care that was taken over the rivers on the way in will be ignored as the returning trekkers plunge regardless into the water. At Confluencia, where a well-earned rest is inevitable, it will be difficult to motivate the limbs to rise up and make that final effort to the road. On the Vacas Valley Route it is customary to make an over-night stop at Pampa de Leñas which is all of 28km from Plaza Argentina. Many will not bother erecting a tent, but will sleep under the stars. Next morning it is only 4 hours to the road at Punta de Vacas.

Other routes

Vacas Valley ascent, Normal Route descent
The best of both worlds, known as the 360-degree route, is to ascend via the Vacas Valley Route and descend via the Normal Route. This provides the time and difficulty on the Vacas Valley Route to acclimatise yet shortens the overall trip by a day. It also allows you to see and compare the two routes.

The difficulty with changing the ascent and descent is that the gear left at basecamp Plaza Argentina must be sent out to the roadhead and returned to Plaza de Mulas. However, if this arrangement is in place with the guide or mule company before the start there should be no difficulty. Mules are making the trips in and out and across every day.

The route between Confluencia and Plaza Argentina
There is a route from Confluencia via Plaza Francia to Plaza Argentina. This involves climbing up to 4800m over Portezuelo Ibañez (also known as the Relinchos Col), before descending into Plaza Argentina. The route is only possible when the level of snow at Ibañez is comparatively low, so would require some advance information. It is a difficult ascent, but a most dangerous western descent, so that a route out from Plaza Argentina to Confluencia is not an option.

Since a porter died descending the col into Plaza Francia the rangers have closed the route.

The Polish Glacier direct traverse
From Camp 2 on the Vacas Valley Route there is the direct ascent to the summit via the Polish Glacier that avoids the Canaleta. The glacier is notoriously unstable and unpredictable, and gaining good grips with crampons and ice axes can be difficult. Nevertheless, the route is direct and consequently much shorter.

From the summit it is possible to ski or snowboard down the Polish Glacier to Camp 2.

Vacas Valley via Plaza Guanaco

There is another route via the Vacas Valley. Instead of turning at Casa Piedra the route continues up following the Vacas river, through Quebrada Vieja Alta (high old valley).

A kilometre out of Casa Piedra there is a significant stream to cross, and then there is a long, flat walk that bends to the west. The river must be crossed again further up the valley. Passing a disused *refugio* at 3435m you eventually arrive at an open area at 3800m which is Plaza Guanaco. From basecamp three intermediate camps will be necessary before the route meets the others below Independencia.

The Plaza Guanaco route is currently closed to protect the wildlife (guanaco). It is a much longer route than the other two, there is little gain in height around the long valley, and there is no rescue service. The only advantage of going this route would that there would be fewer people.

PART 2
ACCLIMATISATION NEAR ACONCAGUA, VALLECITOS AND THE MAIPO VOLCANO

Cerro Tolosa seen from Cristo Redentor

TREKS IN THE ACONCAGUA AREA

PUENTE DEL INCA AND LOS PENITENTES

Getting used to the altitude in a gradual manner is the best outlook. Before heading off on a major expedition check out the local scene. In and around Puente del Inca and Los Penitentes there are gentle, flat walks, and a few arduous ones to follow on.

Andinistas Graveyard

Along the road between Puente del Inca and Los Penitentes there is a graveyard to those who have died in this area of the Andes. The graveyard is immediately beside the road, 2.5km from Los Penitentes and 3.5km from Puente del Inca. It is a sombre place, with many plaques of relatively recent origin. You may walk there and back from Los Penitentes via the old railway or via the mule track.

Natural History Museum

2km along the road from Los Penitentes east towards Punta de Vacas there is a former railway structure that has been converted into a small makeshift museum. This is a fun place, not to be taken too seriously. The owner has used his skills to erect pumps and pulleys to show how volcanoes work. He has rock and mineral samples, and his paintings display the history of the Andes. An illustrated lecture tour (in Spanish, but most will get a good grasp) costs a few pesos.

There is an option of continuing the walk along the road towards Punta de Vacas. At a bend in the road, a few kilometres further on, there is a clear view through the valleys to Tupungato (6550m).

Trekking Paths above Los Penitentes

There are treks up the mountain at Los Penitentes, following the cable car and skiing routes. These will take you as high as 3646m, which is Cerro Cruz de Caña. Simply follow the well-defined ski path up and into the ravine (Quebrada Cruz de Caña), from where the mountain will be seen ahead. Treks up these ski slopes are very popular with those staying in Los Penitentes.

Out of Puente del Inca on the south side there is a trek into Quebrada Blanca. The route is via the first valley on the left on the road towards Las Cuevas. A tough day-long trek will take you to Banderita (3800m), or you may continue up to Cerro Quebrada Blanca which has an elevation of 4411m.

A walk to the Statue of Cristo Redentor

Start/finish	The village of Las Cuevas
Distance	8km round trip
Total climb	700m
Time	Half-day
Terrain	Dirt road
Maximum elevation	3800m
Water sources	No

This is a stiff walk intended as an introduction to the altitude. In the summer months, between January and March, the walk will be over dry ground. Outside of these periods there may be snow on the ground. The area around the great statue is exposed and windswept, and warm gear is essential at all times. Trekking boots are recommended, particularly for the descent. For those not acclimatised expect to take 3 hours for the ascent and 1 hour coming down.

The old border post at Cristo Redentor.

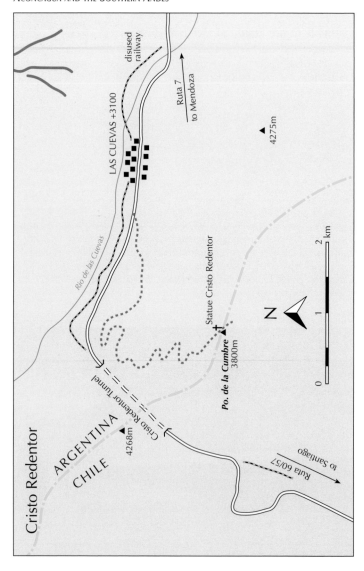

Cristo Redentor

The statue of Christ the Redeemer was built overlooking the pass between Argentina and Chile, and the route to it is the old RN7 road (now replaced by the tunnel). It is accessible with a four-wheel drive vehicle in dry weather, but the route is tough and difficult, and every year there is further deterioration.

To get to the old road it is necessary to go to the village of **Las Cuevas**, which is 12km from Puente del Inca. Las Cuevas boasts an elevation of 3100m. The old road leads off to the south of the village under an arched building. Multiple hairpin bends wind up the hillside.

Cristo Redentor de los Andes

The trek is most rewarding, however, as the col is a very interesting, ghostly place. An old stone building on one side welcomes travellers to Argentina, while close by is another that is clearly Chilean. The enormous statue has many plaques, the principal one signifying the importance of the statue as a symbol of peace between the two countries.

Across the valley is the imposing mountain of Tolosa with its high hanging glacier in the shape of a man with no legs – *el hombre coja*.

The easiest route down is along the steep spine that cuts through the road.

Horcones Valley to Plaza Francia

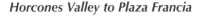

Start/finish	The ranger station at Horcones
Distance	45km round trip
Total climb	2420m
Time	3–4 day trek
Terrain	varied terrain
Maximum elevation	5000m
Water sources	No

The trek is in to the south face of Aconcagua and takes the trekker to a relatively high elevation. It is not a difficult trek. The effort required is well worth the elevation gained and the visual reward is excellent.

Plaza Francia is an ill-defined camp near the south face. It is not necessary to travel all the way in to Plaza Francia to experience the wonderful vista of the south face and the Horcones glacier. Stopping at 4000m will achieve this. However, between 4000m and 4500m is an easy walk over good ground. At this altitude there are many suitable places to camp. Thus, the trekker can vary his penetration up the valley to suit his composure and condition.

The route follows the Ruta Normal from the Horcones Ranger Station, in past the Horcones Lagoon and up to Camp Confluencia. The first day of the trek is easy, and the 15km will be reached in about 3 hours. From Confluencia the trail gets tougher, rising out of the relatively flat Horcones Valley, in and up to the right, around boulders and over rough, steep ground. After about 2 hours the valley widens and the trail is an even gradient over good ground. This good ground stretches from 3500m to 4500m.

The Horcones Inferior Glacier is up to 20m thick in places

There are campsites 6km from Confluencia, not very far from clean water. In the main valley there are ample sheltered sites to pitch a tent. However, up in the valley there is no clean water. Sources of clean water near the

south face are also difficult to locate, depending on the melted water from the face itself.

It would be best to spend the first night at Confluencia, the second at Plaza Francia or an intermediate site, and the third back at Confluencia. Alternatively, it is possible to trek from Confluencia up and back in one day. However, if there are climbers on the south face, it gives little time to watch them.

Plaza Francia is normally deserted, because few climbers attempt the south face. A ruined hut marks the original campsite. At Plaza Francia the enormity of Aconcagua can be experienced. The 2500m high by 7000m wide wall of rock, snow and ice is a daunting spectacle. With binoculars you can look up to the summit. If there are climbers on the face watching them can be interesting. ▸

Detail of the hanging glaciers on Aconcagua's South Face

On the left the great Horcones Inferior Glacier creaks and groans as this living mass works its way down the valley.

ROUTES AT VALLECITOS

Vallecitos is a convenient, practical and inexpensive centre to acclimatise for Aconcagua. This small privately owned ski resort is, indeed, dedicated, during the summer months, to acclimatisation. The proprietor, Alejandro Geras, is himself a high mountain climber and guide.

Vallecitos

Agustín Alvarez 5400m
Quebrada del Salto
Refugio
Junción 5200m
Laguna
Cerro Colorado
Mausy 4800m
Lomas Blancas 3850m
San Bernardo 4450m
Arenales 3500m
Quebrada de la Jaula
VALLECITOS SKI CENTRE
LOMAS BLANCAS TREK
Rincon 5500m
VALLECITOS TREK
El Salto Camp 4200m
Piedra Grande Camp 3500m
Vallecitos 5770m
Río Vallecitos
Río Blanco
Pico Vallecitos 5750m
La Hoyada Camp 4500m
Pico Franke 5100m
to Mendoza
Lomas Amarillas 5300m
El Plata 6300m
Pico de Plata 6100m
Qda de la Angostura
N
Cerro Negro 6152m
0   1   2 km

Vallecitos Ski Centre

Vallecitos is 1½ hours drive from Mendoza, on the road towards Aconcagua. The centre operates transport from Mendoza and to Aconcagua. Due to heavy rains in recent years it is only possible to get to Vallecitos via a four-wheel drive vehicle. It should be emphasised that the mountain lodge is small, generally only able to cater for 40 people, and that the facilities are very basic.

Vallecitos is at an elevation of 2980m. The centre can act as a camp for one-day or half-day treks, or as a basecamp for 2–4 day treks. From the centre there are short treks to 4000m and above, and longer treks to 5700m and even up to 6300m. Guided treks and mule services are available. Alternatively there is a campsite above the centre, with fresh water, with many choices of unguided treks.

The steep road to Vallecitos is off the Ruta 7, the junction less than an hour from Mendoza towards Aconcagua. At Potrerillos a paved road to the left leads towards La Chacrita, then forks right to rise on a dirt track to Vallecitos.

The small ski centre is a motley collection of huts, all shut during the summer except for the lodge. Bedrooms have bunk beds with four separate bathrooms. There is hot water, a public telephone and barbecue facilities. At night a fire blazes in the dining room. There are no frills here – food is simple and basic, and there are no carpets, central heating or televisions.

The campsite above the resort is at an elevation of 3200m on a flat area of open ground known as Las Vegas (the low fertile lands). Vallecitos is a popular area for hill walkers and climbers at weekends. If it is proposed to stay at the lodge, or to go on guided treks, it is advisable to book in advance.

Lomas Blancas (3850M)

Start/finish	Vallecitos ski and mountain lodge
Distance	9km round trip
Total climb	950m
Time	Half day
Terrain	Easy
Maximum elevation	3850m
Water sources	No

This is an easy introductory climb.

From the lodge cross the entrance road and take the route that goes east into a valley, and then turns north up through a narrow gorge. The path winds its ways up to a

The winding path towards Lomas Amarillas and Cerro Vallecitos

col. To the west of the col is the **Lomas Blancas** peak. The peak itself is a rocky hilltop, with a simple metal cross at the summit. ▶

    The return can be via an ill-defined path that goes south from the summit over rock outcrops, eventually coming down over relatively steep ground onto the ski runs.

There are guanacos in these mountains, so keep a close watch.

Cerro Vallecitos (5770M)

Start/finish	Vallecitos ski and mountain lodge
Distance	37km round trip
Total climb	2870m
Time	4-day trek
Terrain	Moderate
Maximum elevation	5770m
Water sources	No

This trek can be varied to suit the weather and the physical condition of the participants. The trek is up towards the snow-capped peaks where there are choices of how far to go and which peak to climb. The most popular choices, on non-technical routes, are Cerro Vallecitos (5770m), Pico de Plata (6100m) or El Plata (6300m) beyond Pico de Plata.

The route is simple, and it would be difficult to go astray. From the rear of the lodge ascend to the northeast, up over the crest, following the river.

    There are four campsites above the Vallecitos centre. The first is at Las Vegas on a flat grassy site at 3200m. The second is at **Piedra Grande** at 3500m, a short walk further into the valley. **El Salto** (the Jump) (4200m) is 3–4 hours beyond Piedra Grande, via a narrow ravine and up over moraine. It is possible to trek from the centre to El Salto, with a full pack, in one day.

At El Salto water depends on the degree of melting snow above, but generally the stream – **Rio Vallecitos** – is adequate.

Top camp is **La Hoyada** (The Pot) at 4500m, 4 hours above El Salto. The route follows the stream as it bends to the southwest. The campsite is sheltered inside an inverted cone-shaped area. Once again water is not too far away and is dependent on melted ice and snow from above.

Summit day to Cerro Vallecitos is arduous. The climb of over 1200m is a long day that should start before 4am. The route is up to the col, then a turn to the right and north. The first peak is **Pico Vallecitos** (5750m). Beyond it over to the north is **Cerro Vallecitos** (5770m).

You can comfortably get back to the hostel from La Hoyada in one day.

The hostel can arrange to deliver a mule load to El Salto. This makes the first day's trek less onerous. Some provisions can be stored at El Salto, so that only the minimum is taken to La Hoyada.

The Cerro Vallecitos summit is an exposed area of solid rock

THE MAIPO VOLCANO

The Maipo Volcano

150km south of Mendoza there is a former old pass between Chile and Argentina beside the Maipo Volcano. Under the volcano there is a lake, known as Laguna Diamante, renowned for its brown trout. If you go there you are guaranteed to come back with a camera full of pictures of guanacos.

To get to the Maipo Volcano requires a four-wheel drive vehicle, or certainly a robust pick-up truck, for there is 60km of dirt track road to pass through. The route is directly south of Mendoza, through the town of Tunuyan, and passing the town of San Carlos. At Pareditas you leave

Brown trout caught in Laguna Diamante

the main road that is heading for San Rafael, and take the road towards the southwest. The dirt track road, due west, into Laguna Diamante is marked. It is not possible to go to the Maipo Volcano on the Chilean side, because the area is a restricted zone.

This wildlife haven is protected, and there are park rangers here. There is no admission charge, and the ranger stations contain information on the wildlife and geology of the area.

The elevation of the lake is 3300m. The summit of the volcano is 5323m. It is believed the lake is a *caldera* where a former volcano collapsed in Quaternary times, up to 5 million years ago. The current volcano arose from this caldera. The approach to the lake is via interesting geological formations, some open conglomerate expanses and some ravines with sedimentary layers that contain fossils.

There are herds of guanacos everywhere, and they are not as timid as those that can be seen in other parks. Here the guanacos have learned to live with the tourists.

The former pass into Chile is south of the volcano. Those who climb the volcano generally make a camp on the north side of the lake. Above this two further camps are generally made, each approximately 600m apart in elevation. There are no technical difficulties en route to the summit. Inka Expediciones is one operator that includes the Maipo Volcano as an optional climb.

PART 3
THE TUPUNGATO AREA

Tupungato 6565m

TUPUNGATO

Tupungato from Friar's Col

THE ANDES' GREAT MOUNTAIN

To the mountaineers of Argentina and Chile the name Tupungato evokes feelings not accorded to any other mountain. Many come to this area to climb Aconcagua – because it is high, they will say, but Tupungato epitomises more of what the Andes is all about. It is a long journey in from the road to get to Tupungato, but it is a journey worth every step, whether it is through the wilderness of Tupungato Provincial Park or through the rugged valleys of Chile's Colorado River.

Tupungato is a dormant volcano and lies on the border between Chile and Argentina, just under 100km south of Aconcagua. It is the 12th highest mountain in the Americas. As recently as 1986 a volcanic eruption was recorded, but this was on Tupungato's little sister, Tupungatito,

which is 5640m and a few kilometres to the south. There is no crater on Tupungato, but there is a smoking crater on Tupungatito. On the eastern face of Tupungato there is a near vertical face, some 2000m high, first climbed in 1985, but tragedy befell the two Argentinean climbers who died on the descent on the southern side.

Tupungato does not attract many climbers, virtually none from abroad. Even with the discovery of the crashed plane in its glacier, when the mountain received world recognition, the numbers of visitors has only slightly increased. This is most certainly due in part to its remoteness.

Matthias Zurbriggen and Stuart Vines were the first to climb Tupungato in 1897. They were part of the Aconcagua expedition led by Edward Fitzgerald.

128

THE MOUNTAIN, THE GLACIER, THE MISSING AEROPLANE AND THE LOST GOLD

A scheduled British South American Airways flight from Buenos Aires to Santiago mysteriously disappeared on 2 August 1947. The British Lancaster was named The Stardust and had six passengers and a crew of four. The colourful characters of some of the passengers fuelled the mystery of its disappearance.

One was a diplomat carrying secret documents from the British king. Relations between Britain and Argentina were tense, and it was considered that the documents, to be delivered to Santiago, were of particular importance. Another was a Palestinian who had a large diamond sewn into the lining of his coat. A German widow was returning to Chile with the ashes of her husband.

The plane had flown from Buenos Aires to Mendoza, and was flying over the Andes on the final leg of its journey. Its route was to circle around Aconcagua before landing in Santiago. The pilot radioed a message to Santiago reporting that all was well, despite a storm over the Andes, and that he expected to land in four minutes. A Morse coded message was then received from the plane, spelling out the letters S T E N D E C. At 5.45pm the plane disappeared, never to be heard of again.

Rumours of the lost plane began to grow. There were reports that the plane, a converted Lancaster bomber, was carrying a cargo of gold. The widow, with her little urn, was transformed into a Nazi spy.

More than 50 years later, on 26 January 1998, two young climbers from Buenos Aires, Pablo Reguera and Fernando Garmendia, were on Tupungato at an elevation of 4500m when Pablo spotted part of an engine on the ground. The engine had the words 'OLLS-ROYCE' inscribed on it.

'How did they get a car up here?,' Pablo mused. The two searched the area and found other objects, including clothing. Pieces of a heavily pinstriped suit were of interest. However, the two climbers did not realise what they had stumbled upon, and the significance of

Army ranger Armando Cardozo and mountaineer Pablo Reguera

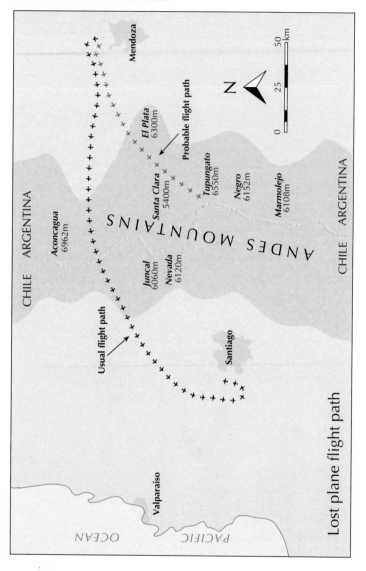

British Lancaster of the 1940s

their find. They took no photographs, and made no record of the location. After a successful summit of Tupungato the climbers descended, casually mentioning their find to the army ranger.

The ranger, Armando Cardozo, asked other climbers to watch out for wreckage, but there were no more sightings. Nine months later Armando was having lunch with an enthusiast of lost planes, José Moiso, when he recalled the incident. José had been brought up near an airbase on the outskirts of Buenos Aires, and had a passion for lost planes and mountaineering. When he was a child one of his father's great stories was about the missing Lancastrian, with its valuable cargo. He had already surveyed the wreckage of a Fairchild plane, which had crashed carrying a team of rugby players.

José persuaded Cardozo, himself an accomplished climber, to accompany him on an expedition. They set off in March 1999, but were caught up in a violent storm, and had to retreat without ever finding the wreckage site. A year later José and Cardozo returned in the company of José's son Alejo. They located the wreckage at 4800m.

Thus began the search that resulted in a major army expedition, of 100 soldiers and as many mules trekking up the mountain, and a flood of international reporters.

Scientific investigations established the aircraft crashed due to navigational error. The pilot had radioed that he was ascending to 24,000ft to avoid a storm. In the clouds, with no landmarks to guide him (and in 1947 positioning systems were non-existent) he had calculated his course and position. He was unaware of a 300mph jet stream and thought he was on course to descend to Santiago when he crashed into Tupungato. The Lancaster hit the mountain and fell onto the glacier. A resulting avalanche covered it. The glacier apparently swallowed up the wreckage and slowly carried it down the mountain. After 50 years it had travelled down, inside the glacier, to emerge at its base.

The fact that neither the gold, nor the diamond were ever found continues to attract those with the energy and ability to search. Some documents have emerged, but they disintegrated before it could be established if they related to important Anglo-Argentinean relations. Among the most amazing discoveries were the aircraft wheels, fully inflated. Ninety percent of the wreckage is still buried in the glacier. Every year it yields up a little more of its cargo.

No one has ever solved the mystery of the Morse coded STENDEC, and no one has ever found the missing diamond.

TUPUNGATO ROUTES

There are four recognised routes up Tupungato:

- via Chile, following the Rio Colorado
- from Tupungato town in Argentina, via the Rio Azufre
- from Tupungato town in Argentina, via the Portezuelo del Fraile (Friar's Col)
- from Punta de Vacas in Argentina, via the Rio Tupungato

All the routes in Argentina go through the Tupungato Provincial Park.

The table below summarises the four routes. The distances include how far the mules can travel. Thus, on the Rio Colorado route the mules go all the way to basecamp (in summer months only). For the routes via Argentina it is necessary to carry all gear for a further 10km approximately. On the Friar's Col route the

SUMMARY COMPARISON OF TUPUNGATO ROUTES

	Rio Colorado	Rio Azufre	Friar's Col	Rio Tupungato
Basecamp	48km	50km	43km	75km
Mule trek	48km	40km	28km/35km	65km
Mule stop	Los Penitentes Basecamp	Portezuelo Tupungato	Friar's Col	Portezuelo Tupungato
Permits	DIFROL, Army, AES Gener	Army	Army	None
Difficulties	River crossing at Mal Paso	Few	Friar's Col ascent/ descent; Rio de Las Tunas crossing	Few
Water	Good sources, but irregular	Good	Clean water intermittent	Good
Total time	12 days	13 days	12/14 days	14 days

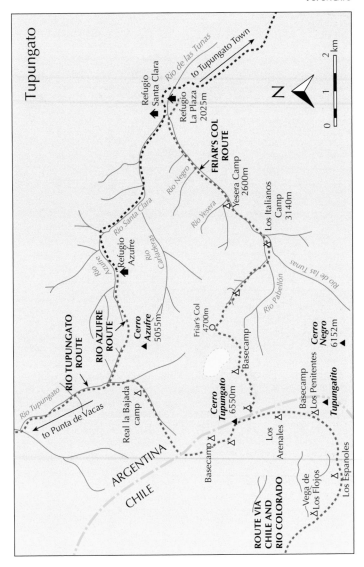

The Tupungato Valley from Punta de Vacas

distance the mules can trek is governed by the ground conditions – too much snow or ice and they have to abandon after 28km, 7km short, 7km that is steep and difficult – so that the total carry could be as long as 15km.

There is a complication. There are two Rio Azufres, one on the Chilean side and the other in Argentina. On the Chilean side the Rio Azufre is a tributary of the Rio Colorado. On the Argentinean side the route follows the Rio Azufre, which joins the Rio de Las Tunas at Santa Clara near the town of Tupungato.

All routes entail multiple river crossings. Via the Friar's Col route, there is a major crossing of the Rio de Las Tunas a few kilometres from the roadhead. The descent and ascent of Friar's Col is semi-technical, requiring ropes and helmet.

Via Rio Azufre and Friar's Col it is necessary to hire mules from the army. The army service is excellent. They will accommodate you and feed you at the roadhead, make great fires, take good care of the mules and act as guides. However, the service is slow and very expensive.

The routes to the summit via Rio Colorado and Friar's Col join on the mountain to ascend on the southern side of Tupungato. The other two routes join to ascend on the northern side of the mountain.

Tupungato via Chile and Rio Colorado

Start/finish	The district of Chacayal, Chile
Distance	96km round trip
Total climb	5000m
Time	12 days
Terrain	Varied
Maximum elevation	6565m
Water sources	Good water sources

The shortest, and the most popular route up Tupungato, is on the Chilean side via Rio Colorado. There are many guides and expedition operators in Santiago who will organise the trek. **Three free permits** are required. The cost of transport from Santiago, and the cost of hiring mules is about half that of Aconcagua.

In Santiago, on Bandera 52, the first of these permits is obtained from Dirección de Fronteras y Limites (DIFROL). You get the second from the army office on Calle Santo Domingo. AES Gener, located at Miraflores 222, operates the power station on the Rio Colorado and will issue the final permit. The sequence of obtaining the permits is important. DIFROL should be your first stop. They will give you a note and directions to the army, and finally AES Gener. All of these formalities can now be done by email. If you email DIFROL first their permit will detail the other email addresses to be contacted. You need to bring your passport for the physical checks with the army and AES Gener.

From Santiago the route is via the Cajón de Maipo, which is southeast of Santiago, through Las Vizcachas, La Obra and El Manzano. You must go into San Jose de Maipo to the army base to have your papers checked and stamped, and then proceed to the gates of AES Gener at Alfalfal. It is then 25km of dirt track up to the start of the trek at Chacayal. En route you will pass arriero huts where you can hire mules. The dusty road is heavily trafficked with lorries from the open cast mine that is across the river from Chacayal.

Early morning view of Tupungato from Piedra Azul

At Chacayal there are good places to camp on grass and there is clean water. You may notice the many holes in the ground here, and you will see them again between Baños Azules and Vega de Los Flojos. These are made by little black moles, which will make or clean out their burrows in the early morning. On this side of the Andes the plants and animals are somewhat different to the Argentinean side, and there will be no chance of seeing guanacos.

The trail from Chacayal is along the right hand, southern bank of the Rio Colorado, along narrow precipitous paths, high above the raging river below. ◄ The first campsite is short of the Rio Museo, which is at an elevation of 2400m. This campsite is known as Baños Azules, and is under the peak of Pan de Azucar (Bread of Sugar). The water running over the bare rock beside the campsite is heavy in minerals and not suitable for drinking. However, below the campsite and further along the trail there is good water.

The second day is a trek to Vega de los Flojos, at 3300m, a tough climb of 900m and 20km. ◄ Leaving Baños Azules the trail rises and falls to cross over the

This initial stretch of 13km requires steady nerves and surefootedness.

Have your shell jacket ready in the rucksack for the trek from Baños Azules to Vega de los Flojos, and expect rain.

136

SUGGESTED SCHEDULE FOR CLIMBING TUPUNGATO VIA CHILE AND THE RIO COLORADO	
Day 1	Santiago to Chacayal and on to Baños Azules
Day 2	Baños Azules to Vega de los Flojos
Day 3	Vega de los Flojos to Basecamp Los Penitentes
Day 4	Rest day
Day 5	Carry to Camp 1 and return
Day 6	Move to Camp 1
Day 7	Carry to Camp Alto, Los Arenales, and return
Day 8	Move to Los Arenales
Day 9	Summit day and descend to Basecamp
Day 10	Spare Day
Day 11	Basecamp to Piedra Azul
Day 12	Piedra Azul to Santiago

Rio Museo via a wooden bridge. Crossing the **Rio Azufre** is energy sapping for there are three ascents and one descent to make. In the not too distant past there were no bridges over the Rio Museo and the Rio Azufre. However, the arrieros constructed makeshift bridges in 2006.

Once the rivers are crossed the trail is relatively uniform until you reach the base of Piedra Azul. This is an alternative campsite an hour or so short of Vega de los Flojos. It is perched above a mound of basalt, and the arrieros have built a shelter here under a rock overhang. It has the advantage that there is a wonderful view of Tupungato from it, but the disadvantage that you must get wet in the morning crossing the Rio Tupungatito. Going all the way to Vega de los Flojos allows for clothes that get wet in the river to dry out in the afternoon, ready for the morning.

There is one matter that upsets this consideration, and that is that it is not unusual for clouds to build and for it to rain in the afternoons between Baños Azules and Vega de los Flojos, which would result in no sighting of Tupungato. Camping at Piedra Azul would assure a wonderful vista of Tupungato in the early morning.

The 'new' bridge over the Rio Azufre

Perhaps in time the arrieros will build a bridge over the Rio Tupungatito, but in 2016 there was none, and the crossing at Mal Paso is an exciting, if not precarious, event. **Vega de los Flojos** (spring of the loose rocks/ground) is a green area, somewhat similar to Piedra Numerada on the El Plomo trek. At 3300m it is relatively well sheltered, has good water nearby, but there is no view of the mountain. You will have noticed the cattle and horses that graze the lands between Baños Azules and Mal Paso, and wondered how they were taken in, and how they are taken out, for the path from Chacayal to Baños Azules is hardly suitable to take cows over.

All the way from Baños Azules to the summit of Tupungato there are multiple campsites to chooose from. Above Vega de los Flojos it is now customary for climbers to make their basecamp at **Los Penitentes** at 4400m. However, there are choices below that, such as at **Los Espanoles**, at 4000m. There is no water available here, but there is at Los Penitentes. ◄ Above Los Penitentes it is usual to break the climb into three stages, making a camp at 5200m (Camp 1), and the second at 5900m, at a place known as **Los Arenales**.

As the name suggests, Los Penitentes is distinguishable by the many penitentes nearby.

Summit day from Los Arenales is only 665m, and is not taxing as summit days go. Expect the day to be extremely windy, with a severe wind chill effect. There are no particularly difficult or technical obstacles to overcome en route to the summit.

Since the final surge to the summit is relatively short, there should be time to break camp and descend all the way to basecamp. The next day can be as long or as short as desired. Some feel it is enough to cross the river below Vega de los Flojos, and make camp at Piedra Azul to dry out, and enjoy a last look at the mountain in the morning. Others will want to make haste as far as Baños Azules. On the way down, there are significant ascents and descents required to cross Rio Azufre.

Baños Azules campsite

TUPUNGATO PROVINCIAL PARK

On the Argentinean side the Tupungato Provincial Park stretches along the Chilean border south of the Mendoza-to-Santiago road. Much more extensive than the Aconcagua Provincial Park, it is a wild, remote region. Herds of guanacos roam free throughout the park and condors soar the skies.

Access to the southern side of the park is usually by taking the road south out of Mendoza, the RN 40, and turning right onto the RP 86 to the town of Tupungato. From Mendoza to the town is a road journey of 80km. There are daily buses from Santiago to Tupungato town. From the road, looking across the plain, there is a spectacular view of the Andes from the Frontal Cordillera with El Plata (6300m) to the Principle Cordillera and Tupungato (6550m).

This charming, friendly town has much to offer the traveller – trekking, horse trekking, wineries, fly fishing, to name but a few. Above all else it is a peaceful place. At an elevation of 1050m it is not quite as warm as Mendoza, and indeed is subject to snow in the winter. There are two good and inexpensive hotels, both on the main street, with the tourist office in the foyer of one of them.

To enter the park it is necessary to obtain permission from the army. The army camp in Tupungato town issues the permit, which is free. From the camp it is 35km over dirt road to where the road divides – to the left and south Refugio La Plaza, to the right and north Refugio Santa Clara. There are three refugios in this area, all of them initially intended as hostels for trekkers, now all army camps. Refugio Plaza is the nearest to Tupungato town and the starting point for the trek via Friar's Col. Over the river, Rio de las Tunas, a few kilometres further on is Refugio Santa Clara. The dirt track carries on past Santa Clara for a further 20km to Refugio Azufre. This is the starting point for the trek via Rio Azufre.

Wilderness trek to Friar's Col 4700M

Start/finish	Refugio La Plaza
Distance	70km round trip
Total climb	2675m
Time	5–7 days
Terrain	Varied
Max elevation	4700m
Water sources	Yes

It is highly unlikely that you will meet anyone else on this trek – no more than a few parties a year seek a permit. Wild guanacos will be seen quite often. Condors and many other birds, lizards and mice, possibly a fox are all most likely. A fire can be lit every night; there is plenty of water and good places to camp. If binoculars can be procured, they will be most valuable for looking at guanacos, condors and for looking across from Friar's Col to Tupungato where pieces of the crashed aeroplane can be detected.

The goal is to climb to an elevation of 4700m at the Portezuelo del Fraile (The Friar's Col), a prominent vantage point where there will be spectacular views of Tupungato and its glacier, and a panorama of the Andes over to Aconcagua. The route can also be used to climb Tupungato itself (provided you are prepared for the descent and subsequent ascent of Friar's Col).

Transport must be arranged from the town of Tupungato, where you will have obtained a permit from the army camp, to Refugio La Plaza. If mules have been hired from the army then they will arrange transport to the refugio. The army will offer the options of them delivering a load to the first or second campsite, taking trekkers in by mule, guiding them and taking them out, or providing pack mules and a ride to a point on the trail. The option of hiring a mule only from the army is not likely to be acceptable.

At **Refugio La Plaza**, at 2025m, the soldiers will be welcoming, probably offering food and accommodation.

Trying to get a signal at Friar's Col

What is possibly more important is to ask for a ride over the River **Rio de Las Tunas**. This fast flowing river is down a gorge, and must be crossed at the start of the trek.

Day 1

Following the right-hand bank of the river, through the gorge, the route is over a grassy plain and up into the valley. The snow-capped peak ahead is Cerro Negro (6152m). The river is murky, a faded orange colour. The route over the next few days will be to follow the orange river, and when a fork in the river is encountered take the right-hand fork. This will lead eventually up to the Friar's Col. The colour of the water is due to sulphur (azufre) deposits further up the mountain.

It is the custom in Tupungato always to leave behind an adequate stock of firewood so that trekkers arriving late in the day do not have to search in the dark. So, even if the stock is high, replenish it.

The **Yesera Camp** is 10km from La Plaza and at an elevation of 2600m. It is immediately after crossing a stream (Rio Yesera, where there is clear water). Look out for a landmark concrete slab and a timber upright – the remnants of a former refugio built in the days of Juan Peron. There will be a store of firewood near the designated fireplace. ◄

If 10km on the first day is inadequate then the second campsite is a further 15km further on, and an alternative site yet a further 5km.

Day 2

The trail continues along the right-hand bank of the Rio de las Tunas until it meets the **Rio Pabellón**. Now it is the Pabellón that has the orange colour, and it is coming down from a valley to the right. We follow the Rio Pabellon on its left bank, where camp **Los Italianos** is situated at an elevation of 3140m. The snow-capped peak now up ahead is Cerro Pabellón (6100m). Firewood can be found up the hills. Around the camp there are tufts of bright green dense vegetation, some turning brown. These are yareta. When they turn brown they are dead, and make good fuel for the fire. The water from the river is murky but quite drinkable.

The energetic may decide to proceed on past Los Italianos to a campsite 5km further on. Casa del Cura is nestled under an overhanging rock, affording good shelter if the weather is bad.

Day 3

This is guanaco day, so tread lightly and have zoom lenses at the ready. The route is along the left bank of the Rio Pabellón until it meets the Rio Ancha, then turn right up Arroyo de la Quebrada Ancha (stream of the wide valley). The trail becomes steeper and the start of the col can be seen ahead. It is wise to be prepared, for the col continues for 7–8km up to the vantage point.

A camp can be made before the first step of the col at 3600m, or, if the weather is kind, up above the first step at 4200m. The first step of the col is steep and may be covered in snow, so that crampons are required. Above this first step there is no water and no firewood.

Day 4

From below the first step of the col to the vantage point is 4–5 hours and 2 hours back. Just a daypack is required. Passing through the long windy col will be slow over

Camp under the first step of Friar's Col

rocky ground. The dip in the ridge up ahead is the vantage point. There is even a place to pitch a tent at the vantage point, although it would be extremely windy.

There is no view of Tupungato, or any other mountain until you arrive at this vantage point at 4700m. Suddenly an amazing vista opens up and you are humbled by the awesome mass and the proximity of Tupungato. The glacier that conceals the remains of the crashed Stardust is clear, and it is obvious how difficult it would be to find a diamond at the foot of the glacier – which is 8km long and perhaps 2km wide. Off to the northwest is Aconcagua. Between it and Tupungato is El Plata (6300m).

The descent down **Friar's Col** is 100m of an almost vertical drop over loose rock. A pair of helmeted climbers, alternating with a rope, could manage to descend, but the subsequent ascent with a heavy pack would be difficult and dangerous.

Days 5 and 6
Retrace your route back to La Plaza. This can comfortably be achieved in two days.

PART 4
THE SANTIAGO AREA

Towards El Plomo summit

SANTIAGO

SANTIAGO CITY

One-third of the entire population of Chile, some 6 million people, live in this sprawling, traffic-congested metropolis. The centre of the city is compact, it is easy to orientate yourself and it has an excellent underground metro. The outer suburbs, however, are disjointed and it is remarkably easy to get lost.

On a clear morning Santiago, viewed from the west, is dwarfed by the snow-capped cordillera of the Andes. During winter, however, it is one of the most polluted cities in the world, because the mountains can prevent smog clearance.

Santiago is more complex in layout than Mendoza. The Rio Mapocho carves the city in two in an east–west direction. The main street of Santiago is Avenida del Libertador Bernardo O'Higgins, also commonly known, as in Mendoza, as the la Alameda. The great liberator himself, O'Higgins, gave this name to it when he ordered the planting of trees to form a boulevard in the French style.

At the lowest point of the curve of the Rio Mapocho is Baquedano, which may be considered the city's hub. The road that goes west is the Pan American Route towards Valparaiso. To the north is the airport and Argentina, and on the east are the Andes.

Every hotel reception has maps of the city. The bustling, mainly pedestrianised, city centre lies to the north of the Alameda, between the metro stations of University de Chile and the rocky heights of Santa Lucia.

Public transport

Public transport in and around Santiago is excellent. The long-distance buses arrive from Mendoza at Los Heroes station. This is also where the bus from the airport stops. From here there is a metro throughout the city and other bus connections to outer areas. It is much more convenient, and of course cheaper, to see Santiago and its nearby attractions by public transport than to brave the traffic by hiring a car. Chilean drivers are undisciplined, swerving in and out of lanes and generally driving too fast. Long traffic jams are common.

The Santiago metro plan is quite easy to understand and has four lines, numbered one to five, with number three missing. Los Heroes is at one junction, whilst Baquedano is at the other, and Tobolaba is on the third. Line no 4A then circles the city to the southeast. Like all metros the directions are given as the last station on the line. The cost of a metro trip is one price irrespective of the distance.

Unlike in Mendoza businesses do not close for siesta in Santiago.

Street scene in Santiago

Handling money

The Chilean peso is quite a different peso to the Argentinean peso, and has been more stable against the dollar than its neighbour. Like Mendoza, it is better to change money into Chilean pesos and pay for everything in pesos. The rates are not as volatile as in Mendoza, and you can safely change in hotel receptions, banks and at dedicated money exchange offices. If you are in Providencia there are two casas de cambio on Pedro de Valdivia.

Making international calls from hotels is very expensive, but all have internet access that will facilitate WhatsApp calls.

For the mountaineer there are many gear shops in the city with everything that you might need for an expedition. The costs are similar to those in Mendoza. There are a few places where gear may also be hired.

IN AND AROUND SANTIAGO

A trip from Baquedano north through Bellavista and up to the heights of San Cristobal (by funicular railway) is worthwhile. There is a good view of the city and the Andes from here. The zoo is also en route.

Near metro station Cal y Canto, beside the river, or not too far from Plaza de Armas, there is the marvellous Mercado Central (Central Market). In the enormous steel supported hall there are wonderful fish restaurants. Not open in the evenings they are filled every lunchtime, especially on Sundays, accommodating up to 800 customers. The menus include fish perhaps never seen in western restaurants. Surrounding the restaurants are endless stalls of fresh fish, fruit and vegetables. The Mercado Central was originally to be a railway station, and the art noveau steel structure was made in Belgium in 1872 and shipped to Santiago.

The El Plomo Inca Mummy, or at least a replica of it, can be seen in the Museo de Historia Natural in the Quinta Normal Park, off Matacana (metro to Estación Central). It should be noted that there are some who are sceptical of the authenticity of the mummy, given that it was in such a prime condition on such a well visited mountain so close to the city, and only discovered in 1954.

A good centre to buy gifts for home is Plaza Artesanos de Manquehue. This is a series of small shops in a covered market on Manquehue Sur, off Av Apoquindo near Las Condes. Lapis lazuli is Chile's semi-precious stone. Lapis lazuli necklaces, earrings, cuff links in silver and gold can be purchased here or in Bellavista. The airport shops charge roughly double.

From the junction of Alameda and Ahumeda in Santiago buses regularly go to the Maipo valley. This long picturesque valley stretches some 70 km into the mountains. There are small wineries for tasting, places to stop and purchase honey, cider and crafts en route, and at the top of the valley there are hot springs (see also the El Morado trek).

A 1½ hour bus journey from the bus station at the University of Santiago takes you to Valparaiso and the coastal resort of Viña del Mar. It can be particularly refreshing to take a walk by the sea after weeks in the mountains. Valparaiso is a quaint old port town with 15 old funicular railways. On Sundays there is an enormous flea market.

Replica of the El Plomo mummy

CHILEAN RODEOS

Chilean rodeo

Every weekend throughout the summer there are rodeos in or near Santiago. To attend a rodeo is to witness a part of the life of Chile. For the purists, Rancagua, the city some 90km south of Santiago, is the home of the Chilean rodeo, and draws bigger crowds to its events. However, the rodeos in and around Santiago give a good flavour of the occasion. In the Friday and Saturday press details of the rodeos are listed in the sports events of the weekend. The rodeo season begins in September, starting with qualifying events, and finishes with regional finals, semi-finals and the grand final in March.

The rodeo is quite different from its North American counterpart. The Chilean version is essentially about horsemanship. There is no wrestling with bulls or bringing calves to earth. Huasos, dressed elegantly with wide-brimmed hats, ponchos and high boots, and working in pairs, chase and control young cows using only their horses. There are no ropes, no whips, and no animal abuse. This is a display of skill and elegance. The judges award points for dressage and for the efficiency with which the Huasos control the cattle.

ROUTES NEAR SANTIAGO

El Morado Valley

Start/finish	Baños Morales
Distance	15km round trip
Total climb	650m
Time	Half-day
Terrain	Easy
Maximum elevation	2450m
Water sources	Yes

Walking shoes only are required on this walk, which is at a relatively low altitude. El Morado is a national park within the Maipo valley, and this walk is a popular one for Santiaginos at the weekends. The walk is through a picturesque valley, where there are many campsites, past natural springs, lots of flowers, particularly orchids, up to a glacier.

Transport to El Morado during weekdays must be arranged. At weekends there are early morning minibuses (7am) from Plaza Italia. Public buses go up the Maipo valley, but stop short of Baños Morales, where the walk starts. The La Cumbre gear shop on Apoquindo is associated with an outdoor sports centre, Refugio Valdes, which is located at Baños Morales, and may be able to help. This centre, incidentally, not only arranges treks, but also has a full range of outdoor activities including horse trekking, fossil hunting, rock climbing and mountain biking.

Through the Maipo valley, passing sports and recreation areas, wineries, waterfalls and stunning countryside, the road goes through San José de Maipo onto a dirt track to branch off for Baños Morales. The lukewarm springs in the village are worth a visit.

LA CAMPANA NATIONAL PARK

There are two approaches to visiting this national park:

La Campana National Park

- a gruelling 1400m climb over
  granite rock in the hot sun, or
- a sightseeing walk through a
  forest where there are many
  rare Chilean palms.

Whichever option is chosen
the park is an enjoyable daytrip
from Santiago. There are many spe-
cies of birds and plants in this wildlife sanctuary.

La Campana is a national park
that lies between Santiago and
Valparaiso. It is part of the coastal
cordillera ridge of mountains. The
dominant peak that can be seen
from every part of the park is Cerro
La Campana (1880m).

There are two entrances to La
Campana national park, quite distinct and separate. To climb the peak, use
the entrance near Olmué, on the southwestern side. From this side no palms
will be seen.

Near Ocoa, on the northern side, there is a second entrance that is close
to the palms, but two days' trek to Cerro La Campana. Ocoa is 1½ hours
by car from Santiago, and a further hour by public bus. Olmué is 2 hours
by car and 3 hours by public bus. The buses to Ocoa do no go to the park
entrances, but stop approximately 2km short. Buses from San Borja near
Estación Central in Santiago go very close to the Olmué park entrance.

At both park entrances there are clear maps that show the various trails
through the forest, where the palms are and where the campsites are located.
A small entrance fee is payable, with an additional cost to camp.

One of the very early visitors to La Campana was Charles Darwin in
1834. He climbed Cerro La Campana (on a cool winter's day) and was over-
whelmed by the 360-degree vista of the Pacific Ocean around to the Andes.

The Chilean palm was widespread in central Chile until it was discovered that it contained a vast store of delicious treacle. Felling of the trees for

151

its treacle was set upon with a will, and, as a result, the tree became almost extinct. It is now protected, and La Campana is the only significant source to survive. The massive trunks are often compared to elephant's legs. Very small coconuts are produced.

The humming bird and the inquisitive truca, with its distinctive call, are birds that flourish in this natural habitat.

There is a small fee for entry into the park, payable to the park ranger at the entrance. Initially the path is steep, but then it levels to an even gradient. En route you cannot fail to notice the profusion of flowers. Orchids and calandrinias are particularly plentiful. A drink from the sulphur springs beside the path will refresh (just a little – the taste may linger). The path eventually leads into a flat campsite beside a number of lagoons.

Cerro Morado is the jagged peak at the end of the valley. It has an altitude of 4500m, and to its left is Cerro San Francisco (4350m) that has a glacier, which sweeps down to discharge its morainic load beside the path. The altitude here is 2450m.

El Plomo (5430M)

Cerro el Plomo, translated as The Mountain of Lead, is the nearest 5000m peak to Santiago, and its white-capped summit can be seen from all parts of the city. The non-technical climb is the most popular in Chile, attracting thousands of trekkers every season. El Plomo gets its name from the deposits of lead that were mined in the area.

No permit is required to climb El Plomo, and no permissions are necessary. Nor do you need a guide. The route is clear and the dangers are few. Invariably there will be others on the mountain.

As part of preparations for Aconcagua El Plomo has much to offer:

The campsite at Piedra Numerada with El Plomo in the background

- the ground conditions are very similar for both mountains
- crampons will be required to cross the glacier near the summit
- summit day is a long arduous day, with possibly 1330m of climbing

The El Plomo trek takes 4–5 days round trip from Santiago. Those with some acclimatisation will have no difficulty in a 4-day trek. For those preparing for Aconcagua or Tupungato an extra day at altitude will be most beneficial.

A number of operators organise guided expeditions up El Plomo, complete with mules. Indeed, some offer the package of El Plomo and Aconcagua as two peaks in two countries, El Plomo intended as acclimatisation for Aconcagua. It is the custom with some of these operators to concentrate the expedition into 3 days, so that the summit day includes the trek back to the first camp. This is too onerous, even for those acclimatised.

Start/finish	La Parva or Valle Nevada ski resort
Distance	40km round trip
Total climb	2400m
Time	4–5 days
Terrain	Varied
Maximum elevation	5430m
Water sources	Yes

The mountain lies 20km to the northeast of Santiago, and is accessed via the valley of the Mapocho river. There are two alternative starting points, both at ski resorts, both at approximately the same altitude, and both requiring a car for access. Public buses go from the centre of Santiago (Escuela Militar metro station or Alameda) via Las Condes towards Barnecha. However, these buses will not travel in far enough to the trailhead. If a group is going a shared taxi will be economical. For those on their own there is a custom of hitching in the area, which will be much more successful at weekends.

The route out of Santiago is via Las Condes and the rather affluent suburb of Vitacura, then into the Mapocho valley, passing the exclusive houses of Arrayan. The starting point at **La Parva** ski resort is on the road beyond Farallones. For the **Vallé Nevada** starting point the road rises steeply after the copper mine, and after numerous hairpin bends arrives at one of Chile's most popular ski centres. At both ski resorts there are hotels, one of which remains open throughout the year. These hotels cater for day-trippers and those seeking peace and relief from the heat of Santiago. They are expensive.

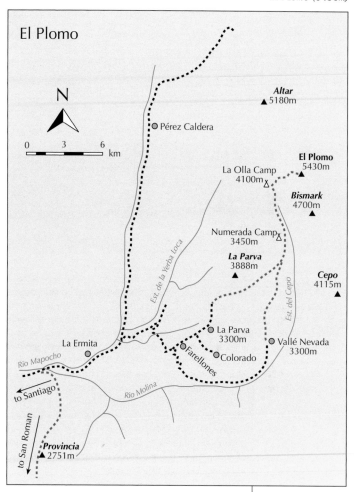

The trails from both starting points join together after a few kilometres to become one trail in to the first campsite. The mules leave from beside the hotels.

Hotel at the start of the El Plomo trek at Valle Nevada

Day 1

Whether from La Parva or Valle Nevada the route begins at an altitude of 3300m. In the summer it will be possible for the delivery car or truck to go up the ski roads to shorten the first day's trek, but this may not be such a good policy for those seeking acclimatisation. The trek in to the first campsite at Piedra Numerada is a mere 3 hours, initially over steep ground, levelling and falling into the camp. From Valle Nevada the route goes directly up the ski slopes, around various reservoirs, following the main river valley.

Piedra Numerada is at an elevation of 3450m, not much of an elevation gain from the ski centre. It is on an open plain, beside the Molina/Cepo River, and there is room here for in excess of 50 tents. El Plomo can be seen clearly up the valley. To the right, dominating the campsite is Bismarck. At 4700m the climb up Bismarck is very steep and demanding, but non-technical.

In front of Piedra Numerada there are springs of refreshing spring water. Around the mighty boulder in the centre of the camp a dry stone wall has been constructed that makes an excellent kitchen. There are plenty of sierra thrushes and wrens about the camp, and the perdicitias call to each other all day.

Day 2

From Piedra Numerada to the second campsite at **La Olla** (The Pot) is a 3-hour walk over uneven moraine. The landscape becomes bleak and barren, with few plants and even fewer birds. En route there are the remains of an Inca enclosure.

Where to make camp at La Olla is a big decision. The best site is beside the orange Refugio Federacion – no more than a tent-size wooden box – at 4100m. There is a water source here, the ground is flat and there is ample wind protection. However, it is 1330m to the summit, a mighty climb for one day.

All sites above Federación are devoid of water. The first is La Olla itself, over the moraine ridge and down to a level of 4200m – hardly worth the effort. At 4300m there is a small, sheltered site with room for six tents. It is on the trail up the mountain. Finally, at 4600m, beside a dilapidated timber hut, Refugio Agostini, there are a few spaces for tents, but the site is very exposed. In calm weather this site would be a good option.

A day acclimatising at La Olla may pay dividends, but any site above Federación is confined and could be exposed and windy.

Day 3 or 4

From Federación or La Olla summit day should commence at 3am–4am. This is aimed at a midday summit when the weather conditions tend to be more favourable. Since the climb will start in the darkness it is good practice to become acquainted with the lower part of it the evening before.

Initially the route is easy. The approach to Agostini, however, is over loose *acarreo* (scree). Leaving Agostini the ground improves slightly, but then deteriorates to resemble Aconcagua's Canaleta. The scree underfoot is weak and makes climbing frustrating.

Delight and elation on El Plomo summit

Before the dawn breaks a look back at the lights of Santiago will make for a welcome pause.

The degree of snow on the mountain will dictate the difficulty of the ascent to the site of the altar. Over a slope that is sheltered from the sun, compact snow or ice may

THE INCA MUMMY

At a height of 5200m there is an Inca altar. It is constructed of dry stone and has an enclosure beside it. On the summit plateau, 200 metres above the altar, there are three rectangular enclosures. In one of them the congealed body of a small boy was discovered in 1954. The body was dressed in fine fabrics of vicuna and alpaca, and wrapped in a blanket. His hair was braided, and on his feet were fine leather moccasins. It is thought that the boy was a sacrifice to the Inca gods. A replica of the mummified remains can be seen in the Museo de Historia Natural in the Quinta Normal Park off Matacana in Santiago.

The site of the sacrifice altar is a moving experience. One imagines the trauma on the mountain, 500 years ago, when a family gave up their little son for the common good. One wonders whether the little boy was held in the enclosure, whether the day was cold, and how he was killed.

require crampons, but will be easier to climb. If there is no snow or ice the ground underfoot will be lose.

From the altar to the summit is a climb in crampons over the glacier. It is possible to shorten the time on the glacier by a roundabout route over stony ground – either way the climb is over an hour, although at first sight it looks like half of this. There is a relatively flat ridge along the summit plateau of El Plomo that is several hundred metres in length. A simple wooden cross marks the highest point. On a clear day, there are stunning views of Tupungato (6550m), Marmolejo (6108m) and Aconcagua (6962m).

Day 4 or 5

An early start the day after summit day allows adequate time to get back to the ski resort and into Santiago by nightfall. The walk is long and the final climb over the hills to the ski slopes will be taxing after the previous day's exertions on the summit. The hotel at the ski resort is quite used to serving dirty, unshaven climbers.

Provincia and San Roman

Along the road in towards El Plomo, just before the bridge over the Mapocho, Puente Lihue, there is a sign, Camino de Naranjo, pointing south. This is the start of a trail that goes over Cerro Provincia, at 2751m, and on to Cerro San Ramón, which has an elevation of 3249m. It is a 5-hour trek from the road to the top of Cerro Provincia, and another 5 hours to the summit of Cerro San Ramón.

These are obviously serious climbs that will require camping, and heavy backpacks to be taken from 1100m at the road up to these peaks. On a cool day, however, it is possible to climb and descend in one day. The route is well marked out. Be advised, however, that there are a few false summits before the top.

From either of these peaks there should be, subject to weather conditions, good views of the city, probably giving a good impression of the smog that the Andes manages to trap.

APPENDIX A

Maps, guidebooks and further reading

Maps

The availability of accurate ordnance maps of Aconcagua was poor, and was non-existent until 2005. Since then a variety of maps have been published. Unfortunately none of them are GPS friendly, being gridded incorrectly or in degrees, minutes and seconds. The best of these is the Zagier & Urruty 1:50,000. The Swiss version by Greulich and Wettstein came out in 2005, but is now out of date. Aoneker Solutions' 1:50,000 is gridded in metric, but using the UTM19N instead of UTM19S, so that it is not compatible with GPS.

Guidebooks and further reading

Aconcagua – RJ Secor's Aconcagua, A Climbing Guide, published in the USA by The Mountaineers. The book was first published in 1994, and has many black and white photographs. Of interest in it are the climbing routes on Aconcagua's south face.

Aconcagua, Summit of the Andes (2006) (in Spanish), written by high mountain guide, Mauricio Fernandez. It is a worthwhile read.

The Bradt Trekking Guide to Chile and Argentina by Tim Burford contains a nine-page chapter on Aconcagua.

Adventure Handbook – Central Chile (2002) by Franz Schubert and Malte Sieber, both German climbers living in Chile. It documents 23 trekking tours in the Chilean Andes. This excellent book is published by Viachile Editores. It may not be readily available in the west.

The Rough Guide to Argentina, by Danny Aeberhard, Andrew Benson, Rosalba O'Brien and Lucy Phillips, 2008; *The Rough Guide to Chile*, by Melissa Graham and Andrew Benson, 2006. Both are excellent publications for getting around countries such as Chile and Argentina.

Chile, by Wayne Bernhardson, is part of the Moon Handbooks series and an excellent guide to the country.

The Highest Alps – A Record of the First Ascent of Aconcagua and Tupungato, and the Exploration of the Surrounding Valleys, by EA Fitzgerald, 1899, published by Methuen, is a wonderful study of the area, despite its age.

The Secretaria de Mineria de la Nación in Argentina published in English, in 1994. A brief paper by Victor Ramos Geology of the Cordillera Principal. A larger, more comprehensive treatise on geology Geologica de la Region de Aconcagua by the same author was published, in Spanish, by Dir. Nac. De Servicio Geologica in 1996.

APPENDIX B

Checklist of essential gear

Head
- Sun hat
- Bandit scarf
- Category 4 sunglasses (2 sets)
- Warm hat

Body
- Dry-flow vests, underpants
- Dry-flow short-sleeve tops
- Dry-flow long-sleeve tops
- Fleece
- Shell jacket with nose shield
- Down jacket (with hood if possible)

Legs
- Shorts
- Trekking pants
- Fleece pants
- Waterproof pants

Feet
- Liner socks
- Fleece or woollen socks
- Trekking boots
- Sandals for wading through rivers
- Triple or double plastic boots
- Crampons

Hands
- Light gloves
- Fleece gloves
- Waterproof, insulated mittens

Other gear
- 35 litre or 40 litre day pack
- 75 litre or 80 litre rucksack
- Walking poles
- 2 water bottles each 800ml
- 1½ litre pee-bottle
- 750ml thermos flask
- Container of food for summit day

Medical/ablutions bag
- Factor 50 sun spray
- Shaver
- Toothbrush and toothpaste
- Hair brush
- Soap and towel
- Disposable wipes
- Disposable handwarmers and feetwarmers
- Headache tablets
- Diarrheal relief tablets (Imodium)
- Saturated oxygen monitor (at least one per group)

APPENDIX C
Guides and mountain services

The Mendoza local government website on Aconcagua gives a list of companies that provide services within the national park, complete with addresses, websites and telephone numbers.

They include only Argentinean companies based in Mendoza. Three Chilean companies, Azimuth360, Chile Montana and Aventuras Patagonicas are very experienced on Aconcagua. There is a fourth, KL Adventure, based in Santiago that organises expeditions, skiing and trekking.

The two largest expedition operators are Inka Expediciones and Fernando Grajales. Inka Expediciones has a permanent team of top-class guides. Inka is affiliated to UIAGM, the first company on Aconcagua to do so. It is also a partner in the Leave No Trace world federation. It operates the Extended Normal Route (Plaza Francia and Cerro Bonete).

Grajales is a second-generation operator. His father, a renowned former climber, was the first to set up services on Aconcagua. With a stock of mules Grajales provides a range of commercial services, including mules and the hire of mess tents, complete with cooks. Grajales hires guides to suit his bookings.

The other main players are Aconcagua Express and Lanko. These four companies all take expeditions up the Vacas Valley Route and down the Normal Route.

Check the website www.aconcagua.mendoza.gov.ar for the latest list.

APPENDIX D

Accommodation and local facilities

The following loose classification of accommodation exists in the region:

Hotel	Bathroom en-suite, stars awarded by the hotel itself, breakfast always included
Suite Hotel, or Aparthotel	An hotel room with a kitchen
Hospedaje	Similar to a hotel, but no single rooms, no telephones or televisions in rooms
Hostería	No bathrooms en-suite
Cabaña	Self-catering accommodation, usually a wooden house. In Chile a cabaña is similar to a B&B
Alberque	Large dormitory style accommodation, not necessarily including breakfast

Set out below is a non-exhaustive list of hotels, where the author has been and stayed. In the major cities there are obviously many hundreds of other such hotels.

The Rough Guides are good references for transport and places to stay, but for places to eat it is essential to have the most up-to-date edition.

Mendoza

Electricity is 220V/50Hz, with two-pin combination sockets, which will take a normal western two-pin plug. Near the permit office, off the main street, on Garibaldi, is a tourist office. The post offices are called Correo and to make a telephone call the Locutorio are inexpensive and efficient. The latter also have cheap and efficient internet facilities.

The unit of currency is the Argentinean peso, but $US are also an acceptable unit of currency. Smaller denomination $US are useful, for it is difficult to obtain change in $US. The peso exchange rate to the dollar has varied from parity in 1999, 3 to 1 in 2000, 4 to 1 in 2002 and has climbed steadily to 16 in 2017. (See also 'Changing money and paying for things' in part 1).

Places to stay

There are numerous hotels in Mendoza, for those on a low budget, to medium priced to luxurious. Inflation has driven

163

the costs per night up considerably over the past few years, so that you must now expect to pay western prices.

Here is a selection of three-star hotels you can find and book online. All of them have free internet access in their lobbies. They are all generally about the same cost. The aparthotels and suite hotels will have a kitchen where you can cook for yourself.

- Hotel Provincial, Belgrano 1259
- Park Suites Aparthotel, Av Mitre 753
- El Portal Suites Aparthotel, Necochea 661
- El Condor Suite Hotel, Leonidas Aguirre 90
- Villagio Hotel, 25 de Mayo 1010
- Montañas Azul ApartHotel, on Peru near Plaza Chile.

The Villagio Hotel and the Montañas Azul Aparthotel are a little more expensive than the others, and are close to the main square, Plaza Independencia. There are plenty of cafes and restaurants in the neighbourhood, such as on the Paseo Sarmiento, a pedestrianised street leading off Plaza Independencia. On the same street as the Villagio, the 25 de Mayo, is the slightly cheaper Corolla Hotel and the Princess Hotel. On the same street as the Montanas Azul, Peru, is the Zamara Hotel, an old style establishment situated between Espejo and Sarmiento.

If it is your style to be as close to the action as possible, and to stay in a cheap, clean, no nonsense hotel, then Hotel Puerta del Sol is a two-star, low budget hotel just around the corner from the permit office and the main street. It is on Garibaldi, off Av San Martin.

There is no room safe, no internet, and an old-fashioned lift. Across the street is a no-nonsense cheap eating house. A hotel very similar is the Royal Hotel Horcones, which is on Las Heras 159.

For low budget travellers next door to El Portal Suites is the Windsor Hotel, and around the corner are the Petit Hotel and the Kapac Hotel. This area of Mendoza is very quiet and is close to restaurants and the permit office.

Hosteling Internacional on Espana 343, Hostel Campo Base on Mitre 946 and Hostel Independencia on Mitre 1247 are alternative low budget hostels.

The Hotel Aconcagua on San Lorenzo 545 is an example of an up-market establishment. Approximately 25 per cent more expensive than the three-star hotels, it teems with North Americans, many on the Aconcagua trail. If you want to stay in the height of luxury you can check out the Park Hyatt on Calle Chile, facing the main park of Plaza Independencia.

Eating out

La Florencia on the corner of Sarmiento and Perú is possibly Mendoza's best restaurant. It is not expensive, and the quality of its food is excellent. The restaurant has its own ranch where the meat is brought from. There is clear glass between the kitchen and the street, so that the food preparation can be seen from the tables outside. Their bife chorizo may rival the best steak you are ever likely to eat. If it is full there are reasonable substitutes down and across the street.

There are a number of large restaurants in the city where there is a set charge and no limitation on how much you can eat. Las Tinajas on Lavalle 38 and Caro Pepe on Las Heras near Chile are examples.

Also on Las Heras at 485, across the street from Caro Pepe, is De un Rincón, a good quality, quiet restaurant. Further along Las Heras at 596 there is the lively Mediterráneo.

On Villanueva between Parque General San Martin and Belgrano there are many restaurants. An example is Torcuato which is an expensive establishment that serves great food.

On Belgrano near Sarmiento there is a fine restaurant called Lasal. It has a large list of the best wines made in Mendoza.

There are two McDonald's, one on Av San Martin near Garibaldi, the other on Las Heras at Mendocinos.

Shops

Av San Martin, the lower end of Las Heras and Paseo Sarmiento are the main shopping streets. There are two Carrefour Supermarkets, one at the end of Belgrano at the junction with Las Heras, the second on Las Heras at Mendocinos.

Mountain equipment

Whereas a few years ago there were a number of outlets that sold and some who hired mountain equipment, the city is now teeming with them. However, the costs are no longer cheap and compare with western prices.

Hiring equipment includes the full range from crampons, double plastic boots, tents, down jackets, sleeping bags to cooking stoves and camping utensils. The rental is approximately 10 per cent of the purchase cost per day, or 25 per cent for 20 days. A credit guarantee is required. For expeditions deals can be struck for an all-inclusive price.

Chamonix are one of the most prominent and flexible for rentals. They are located at Barcala 267 www.chamonix-outdoor.com.ar. Orviz are located at Juan B. Gusto 532 (close to Inka Expediciones). One hundred metres away on the continuation of Juan B. Justo, Las Heras (close to 25 de Mayo) is Aconcagua 6962. You can compare prices by walking between shops.

Limite Vertical is on Sarmiento 675.

El Refugio Adventure Equipment is at Espejo 285, www.elrefugioaconcagua.com.

White water rafting

The Las Cuevas river that collects water from the Aconcagua area becomes the River Mendoza after Punta de Vacas. As it descends into the valley there are centres for water sports, particularly rafting.

The three most prominent rafting companies are Argentina Rafting, Betacourt Rafting and Rios Andinos. Argentina Rafting has its main office in Mendoza on Peatonal Sarmiento 223 Tel 54.261.4290029. It will take clients from Mendoza to its Potrerillos centre (near the Vallecitos turn-off). As well as white water rafting, Argentina Rafting offers trekking, horse trekking and rock

FOREIGN CONSULATES IN MENDOZA		
Austria Espana 948 tel 423 5960	**France** Houssay 790 tel 423 1542	**Italy** Necocea 712 tel 520 1400
Brazil Peru 789 tel 438 0038	**Germany** Montevideo 127 tel 429 6609	**Portugal** Guaymallen tel 451 4179
Czech Espana 1340 tel 438 1592	**Holland** Boulogne Sur Mer tel 423 8565	**Slovenia** Roberto Ortiz (Godoy Cruz) tel 427 1986
Finland Lujan de Cuyo tel 498 9406	**Israel** Olascoaga 838 tel 61 235 940	**Spain** Agustin Alvarez 455 tel 459 0915

climbing. Events are well organised and a weekly programme is set. The centre has a good café.

Vallecitos

There is only one hostel in Vallecitos that operates during the summer, the Ski y Montañas. It can cater for 40 people. The bedrooms have bunks beds, with 4, 6, 8 or 10 per room. There are four bathrooms. The costs are low, but the standard is quite basic.

Los Penitentes and Puente del Inca

The Ayelen is divided into a hotel and a hosteria. Open 365 days a year, the Ayelen's Hosteria will charge under half for a bunk bed in a four-person dormitory, as the hotel of the same name next door. There is quite a difference in the quality of the hotel and the hosteria. Dinner in the Ayelen can be relatively expensive, whereas a meal in the hosteria café is less formal, does not take so long, and is cheaper. The hotel has central heating. The Ayelen hotel is English owned. The owner and his family are very friendly and helpful.

An alternative to the Ayelen across the road is the Cruz de Caña. There are 70 beds here in 3, 4 and 5-bed rooms, and in a large dormitory. The cost is less than the Ayelen Hosteria, and they will operate on a B&B basis, or B&B and either a dinner or a lunch.

In Puente del Inca the Hosteria Puente del Inca has the word Hospedaje over the entrance door. It has 92 beds in 3, 4, 5 and 6-bed rooms, with a bathroom per room. The costs for bed and breakfast, and if desired evening meal, are very cheap.

To contact the army hostel, Ejercito Argentina, you will have to do it in Spanish. The cost per night is very reasonable, including a fine breakfast.

Santiago

Electricity is at 220V/50Hz, with two-pronged round pin plugs. There are a number of tourist offices, one in the Plaza de Armas and another on Providencia.

Places to stay

For the visitor the two obvious choices of districts to stay in are Downtown (or Central) Santiago or Providencia. If you take the public bus from outside the terminal building at the airport it will discharge at the end of the line at Los Heroes Bus Terminal and Metro station. This is Downtown Santiago.

If you search the internet for hotels in Santiago there are hundreds, of all price ranges, all bookable online. The following may be of limited help.

Along Santiago's main street, the Alameda – Av Bernardo O'Higgins – there is the imposing structure of Iglesia San Francisco. This is between the metro stations of University de Chile and Santa Lucia. Behind and beside the church there is a range of hotels. On Paseo Paris there are three hotels, Hotel Paris, Hotel Londres and Hotel Vegas.

Hotel Paris continues in popularity because it is in most guidebooks. However, it no longer has any internal courtyard/garden, is cramped and serves a poor breakfast in a tiny room. Best value of the three is Hotel Vegas. The rooms are spacious and clean, the attention to guests is first class and the breakfast is enormous.

Although this is the centre of town, the streets behind Iglesia San Francisco are bustling during the day with students, but quiet and safe at night.

An alternative hotel location is Baquedano, at the junction of the Alameda and Vicuna Mackenna. This is a very convenient place to stay, and there are a number of hotels.

Hotel Principado de Asturias on Ramon Carnicer has a reasonable apart hotel and a better main hotel. The Principado hotel on Vicuna MacKenna is cheap, but needs refurbishment. All are very conveniently located beside the Baquedano metro. A short walk takes you into the Bellavista district, where there is a public park, a zoo, and a throbbing nightlife of restaurants and street markets.

Hotel Durato on Augustinas is closer to the main shopping areas and even less expensive.

In Providencia there are many hotels suitable for all pockets. At the junction of 11 de Septiembre and Pedro de Valdivia there is the Hotel Neruda. This has a main hotel and an aparthotel. In the laneway to the side there is an entrance that will lead to Hotel Cambiaso Aparthotel which is a small aparthotel that use the upper floors of the building. Rooms are generous and cheap, but no breakfast is provided.

There is a hostel opposite Los Heroes bus station on Tucapel Jimeniz 24, called the Che Lagarto Hostel that is reasonably priced.

Eating out

There are plenty of cafes and bars in the city that serve western and Chilean food, including many McDonald's, for instance on Alameda beside the Univ de Chile metro and on 11 de Septiembre in Providencia. These are open all week, some continuing to serve into the early morning. All of the restaurants, however, close on Sundays and most are also closed on Saturday evening.

There are four restaurant areas in Santiago, Bellavista, El Bosque Norte, Santa Lucia and Providencia. The Bellavista district under San Cristobal is a walk up from the Baquedano metro station, just on the edge of Downtown Santiago. Alternatively, a taxi ride to the corner of Constitucion and Dardignac will be a position where there is a choice of restaurants in view.

La Bohéme is a good quality French restaurant at Constitucion 124. Their crevettes boheme is a chilled prawn cocktail in a tomato sauce. Try the sauté d'agneau a la biére (lamb on the bone), and maybe finish with a trio of sorbets.

El Bosque Norte, near Tobalaba metro, has many western style bars and restaurants, including an English pub, an Irish pub and a German beer garden. The cuisine is distinctly western and so are the prices.

In Providencia, between the Alameda and the river, behind Los Leones metro, there are restaurants with a more Chilean flavour. The Providencia district is compact, and there are also western style, Chinese and other restaurants in the area.

The Santa Lucia restaurant area is mainly centred on Merced and the streets south of it and between Cerro Santa Lucia and Parque Forestal. On Merced there is a small French restaurant, Les Assassins, on one side of the street and La Terraza de Cerro on the other side. The latter serves excellent fish dishes.

Los Buenos Muchachos are a series of restaurants in Santiago that provide meals accompanied by entertainment. These rather large restaurants serve the

Chilean dancing at Los Buenos Muchachos

Donde Augusto restaurant in Mercado Central

best steaks while you enjoy a floor-show of typical Chilean dance and culture. There is one in the suburbs and one nearer the city centre on Ricardo Cumming. They are reasonably priced, and therefore very popular, so a booking is advisable.

To experience a real piece of Chilean life, go to Mercado Central for a fish lunch. Even if fish is not to your liking the experience is worthwhile. Bring a camera. The restaurants are open and particularly busy on Sundays (when other restaurants are closed).

The enormous steel structure of Mercado Central is close to Cal y Canto metro. It can seat 800 customers. Around the restaurants are many bustling fish stalls. Dónde Augusto is the largest of the restaurants in the market. It serves huge portions, so eat the starter before ordering another course. The paila marina is a mixed seafood soup that might be more aptly described as a fish stew. Try the conger eel, and do not leave without tasting the postre of mote con huesillo (peach in syrup).

Acuario is a small restaurant on Paris 817 that is quiet and serves good food at a very reasonable cost.

For those wanting to sample traditional Chilean cuisine pastel de chocho and cazuela de ave are popular in the Santiago area. Barros Luco is a sandwich of thin slices of meat top with melted cheese.

Gear shops

The ChileMontana shop and Andesgear are both in Providencia.

In the El Bosque Norte district there are two shops side-by-side, Patagonia

Gear and Andesgear. They are on the corner of Helvecia and Ebro.

La Cumbre will almost certainly have all that the mountaineer needs, and the best of quality, but it is rather expensive. This German owned shop is on Ave. Apoquindo 5258, approximately 1km beyond the metro Esc Militar on the left.

Doite is a Chilean brand of excellent quality camping and mountaineering gear, from clothes, through pots and pans, to tents. They are all, however, made in Korea.

LIPPI is a brand of Chilean-made clothes that is good and inexpensive. The products are widely available in the gear shops.

Hiring gear is not popular in Chile. Limited sources, however, are available at Patagonia Sport in Providencia. The Federación de Andinismo de Chile, whose website is www.feach.cl, could be otherwise helpful.

Tupungato

Website www.peakware.com is a source of information on Tupungato. It is a receptacle for personal experiences on the mountain.

Those listed as providing services on Aconcagua are generally available to provide similar services on Tupungato.

Chile Montana and Aventuras Patagonicas have guided treks throughout the summer.

There are two hotels in Tupungato, both on the main street, the Hotel Italia and the Hotel Turismo. The latter has the tourist office in the reception.

There are two hosterias in the town of Tupungato, the Don Romulo and the Refuge of the Condor.

APPENDIX E
South American cuisine

Snacks and starter courses

A common *picada* in a restaurant or café is simply *pan amasado* and *pebre*. Pan amasado is home-made bread, generally pitta bread, and pebre is a sauce of chopped hot chilli peppers, tomatoes, coriander and garlic in olive oil. This will often be placed on the table as an appetiser before a meal. *Matambre arollado* is a paté of vegetables and meat.

By far the most popular snack in South America is an *empanada*. This is similar to an English Cornish pastry – mince meat and chopped potato inside a pastry. Variations include some chopped vegetables in the mix. However, the empanada has expanded into cheese (*queso*) varieties and even sweet empanadas. Empanadas are always hot. They are made and sold on the side of the road, sold out of insulated carriers at the border, presented as starters at even the smartest of restaurants. The international fast food chain McDonald's serves empanadas in Santiago.

Tortas are semi-sweet bread rolls. *Alfajores* are sweet cake sandwiches, usually with chocolate inside. *Kuchen* is a fruit pie.

Many sweet cakes and biscuits are made with *dulce de leche*. This mixture of glucose of maize, sugar and milk, is a near obsession in Argentina. It is applied like jam or peanut butter to many foodstuffs – apples, biscuits, even cheese.

Empanadas at a street stall

Meat dishes

In Santiago fish will often be on the menu, but virtually never in Mendoza. Here beef is king. *Bife*, pure beef, comes in many cuts and preparations. *Bife de Chorizo* is the prime form, simply grilled sirloin, or chateaubriand. Bife de Chorizo is a common term in Argentina and in Chile. How long it is to be grilled for is easy – one quarter (*un quarto*), half (*medio*), *tres quartos* or a *punto*.

Carne is meat. *Asado* is barbecued meat. *Estofado* is a stew. *Parilla* or *parillada* is a popular meal in Argentina. The dish is a portion of three different meats – beef/steak, black pudding (*morcilla*) and sausage (*chorizo*), all grilled. Additional servings of the beef/steak are generally provided at no extra cost.

A *lomito* is a steak sandwich, traditionally in pitta bread, garnished with slices of salad, mayonnaise and tomato sauce. In the cities the pitta bread may be replaced with French bread. A *lomito completo* has a fried egg added to the sandwich.

In Chile any meal that is followed by the words '*a la pobre*' (poor man's) will include chips, fried onions and two fried eggs.

A *chacarero* sandwich is very similar to a lomito, but the meat comes in thin, lean strips. A *barros luco* is a sandwich with thin strips of steak and hot cheese.

Arollado chancho is rolled pork. *Riñon al Jerez* is kidneys in sherry sauce.

Fish dishes

Sopa surtido de mariscos is a shellfish soup.

Fresh fish of trout (*trucha*), hake (*merluza*), sea trout (*corvine*) and salmon (*salmon*) are common in Chilean restaurants. Some specialist restaurants will also have unusual varieties on the menu, such as flounder (*lenguado*), tuna (*atun*), conger eel (*congria*) and shellfish (*mariscos*).

Desserts

Postre is the Spanish for dessert. The most common postres are flans, jellies (*gelatine*) and ice-cream (*helado*).

Higos en almíbar is figs in syrup, while *alcayota con nuez* is a syrup of string fruit with nuts.

Drinks

Wine is cheap and plentiful in both countries. A glass may be offered as an alternative to water for a *menu del dia*. *Pais* is a simple, local wine.

Beer (*cerveza*) in South America nearly always comes in bottles of half a litre or one litre. Very similar to western lager the brand names of Andes, Quilmes and Brahma are popular in Argentina, whilst Castel and Estudo are similar brands in Chile. The alcohol content is quite low at under 5 per cent, so mountaineers need have little fear. Red beers, somewhat similar to English bitter, is available, but can be rather expensive.

In the Potrerillos area the brand name Jerome is popular. This beer comes in three flavours – *negra* (black), *roja* (red) and *rubia* (blonde). The rubia is very similar to a lager. The roja could be likened to an English light ale, while the negra has a slightly bitter taste.

Pisco Sour is a most popular aperitif or cocktail, particularly in Chile. It is a mixture of distilled pisco grape juice, egg white, lemon juice and sugar. Pisco wine is made in Chile usually from muscatel grapes.

Chicha is a grape cider, very harsh and high in alcohol content, usually only available in the countryside. In the north chicha is a milky beer, made from maize.

Wine tasting In Mendoza

Wineries in Mendoza

Mendoza is the heart of the Argentinean wine industry, and it is not far from the centre of the city to the vineyards. There is an excellent book entitled *Wine Routes of Argentina* written by Alan Young.

The choice of vineyards is enormous. All of them speak English and wine tours are constantly in progress, although the mornings may be quieter. The Weinert Winery is close to Casa Fader. Chandon, Etchart, Trapiche, Finca Flinchman, Vistalba, Renacer, Mendel and Norton are other choices with international reputations.

These are some of the big names in Argentinean wine. Some of the smaller vineyards are worthwhile too. They will generally not speak English, but have a surprisingly varied choice. This author has sampled wonderful Tokay and Barbera in a small bodega where the owner's products are only for his and his friend's consumption.

Although Malbec is the grape that Argentina has become synonymous with, Bonarda is another grape particular to the country. Most vineyards produce blends that would typically include Malbec, Cabernet Sauvignon, and Bonarda, but also Petit Verdot and Syrah. The harsher grape varieties native to Argentina, and ones to be generally avoided, are Criolla Grande and Cereza. Although Pinot Noir is produced in small quantities in Argentina the taste

173

is not good and unlike any European or North American Pinot Noir.

Ampora Wine Tours on Sarmiento 647, and Trout and Wine at Espejo 266 have set wine tours every day. Some of these take in a tasting lunch where you sample wines that are chosen to complement various foods.

The Norton Bodega (of Norton motorbikes – originally an English company) is en route to Aconcagua. Here you may have a lunch with wines (all Malbec) each to suit the dish course.

Wine tasting in Santiago

Viniculture in Chile is spread over vast areas, unlike in Mendoza. However, there are quite a number near the city itself, particularly in the Maipo Valley. There is no Malbec here, but there is a wider choice than in Argentina – Cabernet Sauvignon, Cabernet Franc, Merlot, Syrah and Carmenére are the dominant red grapes, whilst the whites include Sauvignon Blanc, Chardonnay, Riesling and Chenin Blanc. Pinot Noir is also produced in Chile, though not near Santiago.

The tourist offices in the city will book you into a choice of day or half-day wine tours. Their system is to collect all day-trippers in one central area outside the city and then distribute them into buses on the various tours. Santiago's notorious traffic means you will spend some hours on a bus, so perhaps you might opt for the full-day tour or simply go visit a winery on your own.

At the start of the Maipo Valley is the vineyard of Concha y Toro (shell and bull), now the biggest winery in the world. Entrance to this vineyard is free and a most rewarding experience. The best time to visit is at 10am when there is an English language tour and before the temperature gets too hot. Each participant is given a free tasting glass, allowed to sample three top wines and taken through the vineyard and its cellars. Concha y Toro is renowned for the quality of its Carmenére Reserva.

Undurraga, one of the oldest and most prestigious wineries in Chile is 35km from the city, at Melpilla on the road towards San Antonio, southwest of Santiago. Its dessert wine, which is referred to as late harvest, and made from Sauvignon Blanc, is particularly delicious.

If time or energy are not available for wine excursions there are many excellent wine establishments in the city. Try The Wine House on El Bosque Norte, or Vinoteca Isidora on Goyenechan.

APPENDIX G
Spanish–English language notes

Few ordinary Argentineans speak English, and even fewer Chileans. Those who interface directly with climbers, such as guides, will have a reasonable command of English, but the arrieros, the doctor, the airline official and the bus conductor are not likely to have any English.

On the mountain salutations in Spanish are the norm. For those who are making an unguided expedition, a reasonable command of Spanish is recommended, if not essential. Even for those who have hired guides there will be many occasions when a basic knowledge of Spanish is desirable.

South American Spanish

South American Spanish has some dissimilarities with European Spanish, for instance, how to pronounce words with the letter 'c' in them. In South America the language is softer, less harsh than in Spain (but somewhat the same as in Andalucía). Argentinean Spanish is different from Chilean Spanish, but the Spanish of Mendoza is more like Chilean Spanish. Chileans speak very fast. They regularly drop the 's' from the middle and ends of words, and they use many slang words and words with their origin in the native Indian.

Buenas días will be heard as 'Buena dia'.

Cómo estás as 'como eta'.

Addressing people

In Spain and all Latin American countries there is the formal *usted* and the informal *tu*. In Argentina they also use a third form of address, *vos*. Let's look at an example: a guide I met addressed his father formally with *usted*, whereas the father reciprocated with the informal *tu*. When the guide spoke to the arrieros he used the intermediate *vos*, but when they addressed him it was formally using *usted*. He spoke to me formally, even though I persisted in speaking informally to him. Friends, particularly male friends, will often speak to each other using *vos*.

In Chile the formalities are not so strict, and *vos* is not used.

The basics

The basics of Spanish, however, hold. These will be found in phrasebooks and dictionaries. They include:

- ca, co and cu are pronounced as in English (as in Carmen/cope/culinary) but ce and ci are pronpunced as 's'.
- h   is always silent
- j   is pronounced similar to 'ch' in Scottish loch
- ll   is pronounced like a 'y'
- ñ   is pronounced like 'ni' in onion
- v   is pronounced like a 'b'. However, in many parts of South America the pronunciation is as a 'v'.

Listed below are some of the names and common words or expressions that may be encountered, pronounced in the Mendoza-Chile style, with their English equivalent.

Proper nouns

Words ending in *-agua* such as Aconcagua and Rancagua are pronounced 'aawaa'. There are a few differing interpretations of the origin of Aconcagua. Some postulate that it is derived from the Quechua Language:

Akun = Summit
Ka = Other
Agua = Fearful

Others suggest it is Aymara and translates to Sentinel of Stone.

Other words that you are likely to encounter

Argentina	The 'g' is pronounced as in get
Quebrada	Deep ravine (pronounced 'kaybrada')
Casa del Cura	House of the Priest
Casa de Piedra	House of stone
Cerro Mirador	Mountain viewpoint
Cristo Redentor	Christ the Redeemer
Chile	Pronounced 'Chillay'
Las Cuevas	The Caves
Cordón del Plata	The string or line of the Silver
Cresta del Viento	Windy Crest
Ejercito	Army (pronounced 'ehersito')
Estancia	Ranch or farm
La Hoyada	The pit, pothole
Mendoza	Pronounce the 'z' as in English
Lomas Blancas	White hills

La Olla	The cooking pot (pronounced 'oya')
Pabellón	Pavilion, tent (pronounced 'pabeyon')
Penitentes	Standing icicles
Plata	Silver
Plomo	Lead (metal)
Portezuelo de Fraile	Col of the Friar
Punta de Vacas	The point of (the river of) cows
Puente del Inca	Bridge of the Incas
Pampa de Leñas	Plains where there is firewood
Rocas Blancas	White Rocks
El Salto	The jump or leap
Valle de Las Vacas	Valley of the Cows (pronounced 'bayay de las bacas')
Vallecitos	Little valleys (pronounced 'bayaysitos')

Salutations

hola	hello
buenos días	good day/good morning
buenas tardes	good afternoon
buenas noches	good evening/night
adíos	goodbye
hasta luego	see you later
cómo estás	how are you?
muy bien, y tú	very good, and you?
buen provecho	bon appétit

Numbers

0	*cero*
1	*uno*
2	*dos*
3	*tres*
4	*cuatro*
5	*cinco*
6	*seis*
7	*siete*

8	*ocho*
9	*nueve*
10	*diez*
11	*once*
12	*doce*
13	*trece*
14	*catorce*
15	*quince*
16	*dieciséis*
17	*diecisiete*
18	*dieciocho*
19	*diecinueve*
20	*veinte*
21	*veintiuno*
29	*veintinueve*
30	*treinta*
32	*treinta y dos*
40	*cuarenta*
50	*cincuenta*
60	*sesanta*
70	*setenta*
80	*ochenta*
90	*noventa*
100	*cien*
110	*ciento diez*
500	*quinientos*
1000	*mil*
2000	*dos mil*
million	*un millón*

Days

Monday	*lunes*
Tuesday	*martes*
Wednesday	*miércoles*
Thursday	*jueves*
Friday	*viernes*
Saturday	*sábado*
Sunday	*domingo*

THE ALPHABET

Letter	Phonetic alphabet	Pronounced
A	Aconcagua	'a'
B	Bilbao	'be'
C	Carmen	'ce'
Ch	Champiñon	'che'
D	Deportivo	'de'
E	Español	'e'
F	Francia	'efe'
G	Go	'khe'
H	Hasta	'aache'
I	Isabel	'ee'
J	José	'khota'
K	Kilo	'ka'
L	Londres	'ele'
Ll	Tortilla	'elye'
M	Metro	'eme'
N	Noches	'ene'
O	Otro	'o'
P	Puente	'pe'
Q	Quisiera	'koo'
R	Río	'ere'
S	Sábado	'ese'
T	Tardes	'te'
U	Uno	'oo'
V	Viento	'oobay'
W	Washington	'oobay doblay'
X	Taxi	'ekees'
Y	Paraquay	'eegriayge'
Z	Zeta	'theta'

Months

January	*enero*
February	*febrero*
March	*marzo*
April	*abril*
May	*mayo*
June	*junio*
July	*julio*
August	*agosto*
September	*septiembre*
October	*octubre*
November	*noviembre*
December	*diciembre*

Seasons

spring	*la primavera*
summer	*el verano*
autumn	*el otoño*
winter	*el invierno*

Colours

black	*negro*
blue	*azul*
brown	*marrón*
cream	*crema*
gold	*dorado*
green	*verde*
grey	*gris*
orange	*naranja*
red	*rojo*
silver	*plateado*
white	*blanco*
yellow	*amarillo*

Shapes

big	*grande*
fat	*gordo/a*
flat	*llano/a*
long	*largo/a*
narrow	*estrecho/a*
round	*redondo/a*
small	*pequeño/a*

tall	*alto/a*
thin	*delgado*
tiny	*pequeñito*

Food

apple	*la manzana*
avocado	*aguacate* (but in Chile *palta*)
banana	*la plátano*
biscuits	*las galletas*
bread	*el pan*
bread roll	*el panecillo*
butter	*la mantequilla* (*manteca* in Argentina)
cheese	*el queso*
chicken	*el pollo*
chips	*las papas fritas*
eggs	*los huevos*
garlic	*la ajo*
ham	*el jamón*
honey	*la miel*
jam	*la marmelada*
marmalade	*la marmelada de naranja*
milk	*la leche*
mushrooms	*los champiñones*
mustard	*la mostaza*
onion	*la cebolla*
pepper	*la pimienta*
potatoes	*las papas*
prawns	*las gambas*
rice	*el arroz*
salt	*la sal*
steak	*el bistec* or *bife*
stew	*el estofado*
a portion of…	*una ración de…*
breakfast	*el desayuno*
lunch	*el almuerzo*
dinner	*la cena*
plate	*el plato*
boiled	*hervido*
fried	*frito*

grilled	*a la parrilla*
roast	*asado*
scrambled	*revueltos*
stewed	*cocido, guisado*
rare	*poco hecho, or uno quarto*
medium	*normal, or medio*
medium to	
well done	*trés quartos*
well done	*bien hecho, or a punto*
menu	*la carta*
set menu	*el menu del día*

Words particular to mountains

acarreo	lose stones, scree
aceite bronceador	suntan oil
altura	altitude, height
ampolla	blister
aseos	toilets
baños	toilets
botella	bottle
brújula	compass
cabalgata	trekking on horseback
caminata	trek
camping	campsite
casco	helmet
cerro	mountain
cima, cumbre	summit
colchón neumático	air bed
congelado	frozen
cordillera	mountain range
dedos	fingers
dedo del pie	toe
despacio	slowly
dolor de cabeza	headache
este	east
excusado	toilet
gafas de sol	sunglasses
helada	frost
linterna	torch
lugar de campamento	campsite
neblina	mist

nieve	snow
norte	north
nube	cloud
oeste	west
peligro	danger
pie	foot
precipicio	cliff
rappel	descent by rope
refugio	shelter
resbaladizo	slippery
ripio	dirt-track road
saco de dormir	sleeping bag
sur	south
siga derecho	keep straight ahead
tienda de deportes	sports shop

Not spanish

A *bocadillo* may be a sandwich in Spain, but it is a mixed food ball, generally vegetable, in South America. Sandwich is the common term here. A *bocadillo de acelga* is a ball mixture of chopped vegetables, cheese and garlic. A *bocadito* is a small item of food, generally a piece of chocolate taken with coffee.

There are no *tapas* (snacks at a bar or before a meal), but you may be served *picadas* instead. These are the region's tapas equivalent.

Mantequilla is butter in Spain and in Chile, but *manteca* is the more common name in Argentina.

Aqui and *alli* are Spanish for here and there, but in Chile they use *aca* and *alla*.

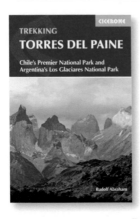
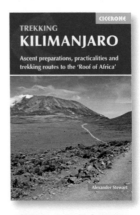

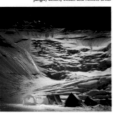
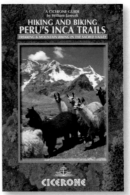

LISTING OF CICERONE GUIDES

SCOTLAND
Backpacker's Britain:
Northern Scotland
Ben Nevis and Glen Coe
Cycling in the Hebrides
Great Mountain Days in Scotland
Mountain Biking in Southern and
Central Scotland
Mountain Biking in West and
North West Scotland
Not the West Highland Way
Scotland
Scotland's Best Small Mountains
Scotland's Far West
Scotland's Mountain Ridges
Scrambles in Lochaber
The Ayrshire and Arran
Coastal Paths
The Border Country
The Cape Wrath Trail
The Great Glen Way
The Great Glen Way Map Booklet
The Hebridean Way
The Hebrides
The Isle of Mull
The Isle of Skye
The Skye Trail
The Southern Upland Way
The Speyside Way
The Speyside Way Map Booklet
The West Highland Way
Walking Highland Perthshire
Walking in Scotland's Far North
Walking in the Angus Glens
Walking in the Cairngorms
Walking in the Ochils, Campsie
Fells and Lomond Hills
Walking in the Pentland Hills
Walking in the Southern Uplands
Walking in Torridon
Walking Loch Lomond and
the Trossachs
Walking on Arran
Walking on Harris and Lewis
Walking on Jura, Islay
and Colonsay
Walking on Rum and the
Small Isles
Walking on the Orkney and
Shetland Isles
Walking on Uist and Barra
Walking the Corbetts Vol 1
Walking the Corbetts Vol 2
Walking the Galloway Hills
Walking the Munros Vol 1
Walking the Munros Vol 2
West Highland Way Map Booklet

Winter Climbs Ben Nevis and
Glen Coe
Winter Climbs in the Cairngorms

NORTHERN ENGLAND TRAILS
Hadrian's Wall Path
Hadrian's Wall Path Map Booklet
Pennine Way Map Booklet
The Coast to Coast Walk
The Coast to Coast Map Booklet
The Dales Way
The Pennine Way

LAKE DISTRICT
Cycling in the Lake District
Great Mountain Days in the
Lake District
Lake District Winter Climbs
Lake District:
High Level and Fell Walks
Lake District:
Low Level and Lake Walks
Lakeland Fellranger
Mountain Biking in the
Lake District
Scafell Pike
Scrambles in the Lake District
– North
Scrambles in the Lake District
– South
Short Walks in Lakeland
Book 1: South Lakeland
Short Walks in Lakeland
Book 2: North Lakeland
Short Walks in Lakeland
Book 3: West Lakeland
Tour of the Lake District
Trail and Fell Running in the
Lake District

NORTH WEST ENGLAND
AND THE ISLE OF MAN
Cycling the Pennine Bridleway
Isle of Man Coastal Path
The Lancashire Cycleway
The Lune Valley and Howgills
The Ribble Way
Walking in Cumbria's Eden Valley
Walking in Lancashire
Walking in the Forest of Bowland
and Pendle
Walking on the Isle of Man
Walking on the West
Pennine Moors
Walks in Lancashire
Witch Country
Walks in Ribble Country
Walks in Silverdale and Arnside

NORTH EAST ENGLAND,
YORKSHIRE DALES
AND PENNINES
Cycling in the Yorkshire Dales
Great Mountain Days in
the Pennines
Historic Walks in North Yorkshire
Mountain Biking in the
Yorkshire Dales
South Pennine Walks
St Oswald's Way and
St Cuthbert's Way
The Cleveland Way and the
Yorkshire Wolds Way
The Cleveland Way Map Booklet
The North York Moors
The Reivers Way
The Teesdale Way
Walking in County Durham
Walking in Northumberland
Walking in the North Pennines
Walking in the Yorkshire Dales:
North and East
Walking in the Yorkshire Dales:
South and West
Walks in Dales Country
Walks in the Yorkshire Dales

WALES AND WELSH BORDERS
Glyndwr's Way
Great Mountain Days
in Snowdonia
Hillwalking in Shropshire
Hillwalking in Wales – Vol 1
Hillwalking in Wales – Vol 2
Mountain Walking in Snowdonia
Offa's Dyke Path
Offa's Dyke Map Booklet
Pembrokeshire Coast Path
Map Booklet
Ridges of Snowdonia
Scrambles in Snowdonia
The Ascent of Snowdon
The Ceredigion and Snowdonia
Coast Paths
The Pembrokeshire Coast Path
The Severn Way
The Snowdonia Way
The Wales Coast Path
The Wye Valley Walk
Walking in Carmarthenshire
Walking in Pembrokeshire
Walking in the Forest of Dean
Walking in the South
Wales Valleys
Walking in the Wye Valley
Walking on the Brecon Beacons

For full information on all our guides, books and eBooks, visit our website:
www.cicerone.co.uk

Walking – Trekking – Mountaineering – Climbing – Cycling

Over 40 years, Cicerone have built up an outstanding collection of over 300 guides, inspiring all sorts of amazing adventures.

Every guide comes from extensive exploration and research by our expert authors, all with a passion for their subjects. They are frequently praised, endorsed and used by clubs, instructors and outdoor organisations.

All our titles can now be bought as **e-books**, **ePubs** and **Kindle** files and we also have an online magazine – **Cicerone Extra** – with features to help cyclists, climbers, walkers and trekkers choose their next adventure, at home or abroad.

Our website shows any **new information** we've had in since a book was published. Please do let us know if you find anything has changed, so that we can publish the latest details. On our **website** you'll also find great ideas and lots of detailed information about what's inside every guide and you can buy **individual routes** from many of them online.

It's easy to keep in touch with what's going on at Cicerone by getting our monthly **free e-newsletter**, which is full of offers, competitions, up-to-date information and topical articles. You can subscribe on our home page and also follow us on **Facebook** and **Twitter** or dip into our **blog**.

Cicerone – the very best guides for exploring the world.

CICERONE

Juniper House, Murley Moss, Oxenholme Road, Kendal, Cumbria LA9 7RL
Tel: 015395 62069 info@cicerone.co.uk
www.cicerone.co.uk and **www.cicerone-extra.com**